STRATEGIZING THE RUSSIAN GAS INDUSTRY

The Far Eastern Vector

STRATEGIZING THE RUSSIAN GAS INDUSTRY

The Far Eastern Vector

(Monograph)

by

Nikita I. Sasaev, PhD (Economics)

Editorial Research Supervisors:

Sergey M. Darkin, PhD (Economics) and Vladimir L. Kvint, PhD (Economics)

AAP | APPLE ACADEMIC PRESS

First edition published 2024

Apple Academic Press Inc.
1265 Goldenrod Circle, NE,
Palm Bay, FL 32905 USA

760 Laurentian Drive, Unit 19,
Burlington, ON L7N 0A4, CANADA

CRC Press
2385 NW Executive Center Drive,
Suite 320, Boca Raton FL 33431

4 Park Square, Milton Park,
Abingdon, Oxon, OX14 4RN UK

Library and Archives Canada Cataloguing in Publication

Title: Strategizing the Russian gas industry : the Far Eastern vector (monograph) / by Nikita I. Sasaev, PhD (economics); editorial research supervisors: Sergey M. Darkin, PhD (economics) and Vladimir L. Kvint, PhD (economics).
Names: Sasaev, N. I. (Nikita Igorevich), author.
Description: First edition. | Series statement: Strategy of the Russian Far East library | Includes bibliographical references and index.
Identifiers: Canadiana (print) 20240372948 | Canadiana (ebook) 20240372972 | ISBN 9781774919347 (hardcover) | ISBN 9781774919354 (softcover) | ISBN 9781003499886 (ebook)
Subjects: LCSH: Gas industry—Russia (Federation)—Russian Far East—Methodology.
Classification: LCC HD9581.R92 S27 2024 | DDC 338.2/728509474—dc23

Library of Congress Cataloging-in-Publication Data

CIP data on file with US Library of Congress

ISBN: 978-1-77491-934-7 (hbk)
ISBN: 978-1-77491-935-4 (pbk)
ISBN: 978-1-00349-988-6 (ebk)

About the Author

Nikita I. Sasaev, PhD (Economics)
Associate Professor, Economic and Financial Strategy Department, Moscow School of Economics, Lomonosov Moscow State University, Russia

Nikita I. Sasaev, PhD (Econ.), is an Associate Professor at the Economic and Financial Strategy Department at Moscow School of Economics, Lomonosov Moscow State University. For more than five years, he has been conducting research in the field of industrial strategizing, primarily in the gas industry. He has more than 25 published research papers in this field. In addition, the author is directly involved in the development and implementation of a number of practical strategies.

About the Editorial Research Supervisors

Sergey M. Darkin, PhD (Economics)
Former Governor, Primorsky Region of the Russian Federation; Former Deputy Minister, Regional Development of the Russian Federation; President, Pacific Investment Group (TIGR)

Sergey M. Darkin, PhD (Econ.), was the Governor of the Primorsky Region of the Russian Federation from 2001 to 2012, Deputy Minister of Regional Development of the Russian Federation from 2012 to 2014, and is currently President of the Pacific Investment Group (TIGR) since 2014. Dr. Darkin currently serves as a board member of several leading companies and banks. He is an authority on issues of Asia-Pacific economic development and a well-established professional in regional cooperation and the shipping and fishing industries, among other areas.

Vladimir L. Kvint, PhD (Economics)
Chair, Economic and Financial Strategy Department, Moscow School of Economics at Lomonosov Moscow State University; Research Director, Center for Strategic Studies, Institute of Complex Systems Mathematical Research (CSS ICSMR)

Vladimir L. Kvint, Dr.Sc. (Econ.), has been Professor of Strategy, Management Systems and International Economics at Fordham University, New York University's Stern School of Business, American and LaSalle Universities, and Babson College and serves as Chair of the Economic and Financial Strategy Department in the Moscow School of Economics at Lomonosov Moscow State University. He is also Research Director at the Center for Strategic Studies at the Institute of Complex Systems Mathematical Research (CSS ICSMR). Dr. Kvint is a member of the Bretton Woods Committee, a lifetime Foreign Member of the Russian Academy of Science, a U.S. Fulbright Scholar, and a well-established strategic advisor.

Contents

About the Book

In non-stationary economic conditions, the Far Eastern Federal District, as one of the most promising macro-regions of Russia, despite the presence of accumulated problems, has the necessary resources and technological potential for a breakthrough in socio-economic development. In the Russian Far East, a potential driver of development can be the gas industry, the functioning and development of which the entire spectrum of interests is concentrated, and which has a number of large-scale strategic opportunities. The implementation of the identified opportunities by individual projects in most cases will bring only a single and short-term success, in this regard, an integrated approach is necessary, providing for the development and further implementation of a full-fledged industrial strategy integrated into the general strategy system.

The research is based on the general theory of Strategy and strategizing methodology developed by the Center for Strategic Research at the Institute of Mathematical Research of Complex Systems and the Economic and Financial Strategy Department at Moscow School of Economics at Lomonosov Moscow State University with the leadership of Foreign Member of the Russian Academy of Sciences, professor Vladimir L. Kvint.

The monograph aims to form the concept of the Russian Far East gas industry strategy, taking into account the entire range of interests, strategic trends, and opportunities. Based on the results of a comprehensive strategic analysis, the concept of the mission and vision of the Russian Far East gas industry strategy is formed, and the strategic priorities are disclosed in detail, indicating the resulting goals and the main effects of public and economic efficiency from their implementation.

Preface

The Russian Far East is a unique macro-region of the Russian Federation, the strategic importance of which is rapidly growing. The largest region of Russia in terms of territory has colossal natural resources and strategic proximity to the rapidly developing countries of the Asia-Pacific region. An extensive mineral resource base and fuel and energy sector are together a significant strategic factor in ensuring the economic prosperity of the Russian Far East in the long term. The large-scale industrial development of multicomponent natural gas fields and the concentration of diverse interest groups around the industrial processes being built strengthen the interest in the strategic development of the Far Eastern gas industry in order to accelerate the socio-economic development of the Russian Far East. *Strategizing the Russian Gas Industry: The Far Eastern Vector* by Nikita I. Sasaev aims to do just that.

In addition to conducting active research activities on industrial strategizing, the author, who is an Associate Professor at the Economic and Financial Strategy Department at Lomonosov Moscow State University's Moscow School of Economics, is directly involved in the development and implementation of a number of practical strategies, which increases the practicality of the results obtained in this research.

The author begins the book with a description of the theoretical and methodological basis of the research, presenting the methodological foundations and stages of strategizing the Russian Far East gas industry and, in particular, the formation of the gas strategy concept. The second chapter is devoted to the study of the initial potential and development trajectory, where the author presents the results of strategic diagnostics of the Far Eastern gas industry as an object of strategy in six areas.

The author attaches particular importance to determining where the Far Eastern Federal District's (FEFD) gas industry strategy fits within the hierarchy of strategies, as well as to analyzing and accounting for interests focused on the functioning and development of this industry in the region. Thus, in the third chapter, the vertical and horizontal interrelations of the Far Eastern gas industry within the general system of strategies are analyzed, and the main interest groups (national, public, regional, industrial, corporate, international) are systematized, which the author takes into account when conducting subsequent strategic analysis and conceptualization of the main elements of the Russian Far East gas industry strategy.

The fourth and fifth chapters are aimed at a comprehensive strategic analysis of trends and the search and justification of strategic opportunities for the development of the Far Eastern gas industry. The results of which the author uses in the sixth chapter form his concept of strategy, namely the mission and vision.

As a result, the author proposes the concepts of six large-scale strategic priorities, supported by competitive advantages and resource opportunities, which have a specific goal and result in public and economic effects. All of these priorities are aimed at realizing the accumulated potential of the Far Eastern gas industry in the context of the multiplicative stimulation of the socio-economic development of each of the regions of the Far Eastern Federal District and the Russian macro-region as a whole for the period up to 2035 and beyond.

This monograph by Nikita I. Sasaev makes a significant scientific and practical contribution to the study of the long-term prospects for the development of the Russian Far East, namely, to substantiate the strategic priorities of the Far Eastern gas industry through the lens of the socio-economic development of the entire macro-region. This book continues the series of books that make up the Strategy of the Russian Far East Library, which has been published since 2015.

—Sergey M. Darkin, PhD

Vladimir L. Kvint, Dr.Sc.

Introduction

The ever-changing nature of global and regional economic systems, coupled with the increasing instability caused by various emerging trends, not only leads to structural changes in the economy but also triggers social transformations. These factors collectively emphasize the significance and complexity of achieving strategic goals to ensure the socio-economic development of both the Russian regions and the nation as a whole. However, this complexity is largely attributed to the diminishing availability of resources, limited access to advanced technical and technological support, and heightened interregional competition for economic factors. Some of these trends hold strategic importance for fostering innovative economic development.

Even amidst the aforementioned conditions, the Russian Far Eastern Federal District (FEFD) stands out as one of the most promising macro-regions in Russia, despite the presence of existing challenges. This region possesses the necessary resources and technological potential to make a significant breakthrough in socio-economic development. It has been repeatedly acknowledged that this breakthrough can be achieved through the implementation of large-scale projects and fundamental transformations. In this regard, particular attention should be directed towards the establishment of industrial drivers, which involve utilizing the existing regional and industrial potential to stimulate long-term socio-economic development in a multiplicative manner.

The outcomes of the strategic analysis have revealed that the Russian Far East gas industry holds the potential to act as a driving force, concentrating a wide range of interests at the national, public, regional, industry, corporate, and international levels. Moreover, this industry presents numerous significant strategic opportunities on a large scale.

However, the author argues that pursuing the identified opportunities through individual projects will, in most cases, only yield isolated and short-term success. Therefore, an integrated approach is necessary, which entails the development and subsequent implementation of a comprehensive industrial strategy that is seamlessly integrated into the General System of Strategies.

In line with this objective, the purpose of this monograph is to systematically organize the results of the strategic analysis conducted on the Russian Far East gas industry and formulate a concept for an industrial strategy based on these findings.

CHAPTER 1

The Theoretical and Methodological Basis for Strategizing the Russian Far East Gas Industry

1.1 THEORETICAL AND METHODOLOGICAL PROVISIONS FOR THE FORMATION OF THE RUSSIAN FAR EAST GAS INDUSTRY STRATEGY CONCEPT

This scientific research is based on the general theory of strategy and strategizing methodology developed by the Center for Strategic Research at the Institute of Mathematical Research of Complex Systems and the Economic and Financial Strategy Department at Moscow School of Economics at Lomonosov Moscow State University under the leadership of Dr. Vladimir L. Kvint [1, 2]. Built on the fundamental principles of strategic mind and other important philosophical theories, and incorporating many years of scientific and practical experience [3–5], it has repeatedly demonstrated its viability and effectiveness in strategizing completely different areas and objects [6].

Industrial strategizing is one of these areas that demonstrates its viability, although it requires accounting for specifics and the use of additional methodological tools to the primary one. These were developed and personally tested by the author of this monograph. An industrial strategy, like any other, is a complex document that includes an integral system of interconnected blocks and elements [4]. The emphasis on developing the industrial strategy concept for the Russian Far East gas industry in this study is based on the fact that it is this core block of elements that is decisive at the entire stage of strategizing up to its full implementation.

Strategizing the Russian Gas Industry: The Far Eastern Vector. Nikita I. Sasaev (Ed)

In turn, the industrial strategy concept should include two interdependent elements [7]: *mission* and *vision*.

The mission of the Russian Far East gas industry strategy, in addition to providing strategically significant information about the industrial strategizing object (such as causes of occurrence and validity of operation and development), should establish the general goal and determine the usefulness of the strategy in the context of appreciating the diversity of interest groups included in the process of development and operation of the object [8]. In addition, the mission should contribute to the Far Eastern Federal District subjects' confidence in the implementation of their long-term interests, as well as designate attractiveness for potential investors, which is not only one of the principles for the effective implementation of the future strategy but also one of the most important factors in the economic development of the region as a whole [9, 10].

The vision of the Russian Far East gas industry strategy, in accordance with the strategizing methodology, should regulate the system of strategic principles that ensure the effectiveness of its development and implementation [10, 11] and contain the concepts of strategic priorities formulated on the basis of identified and justified strategic opportunities, as well as supported by an appropriate resource base and competitive advantages [5]. In addition, for each of the strategic priorities, the resulting goal and potential public and economic efficiency should be indicated [12, 13], which in the future will allow tracking of the process of their implementation, for example, by economic and mathematical modeling [14, 15] or econometric analysis [16].

To form a practical and effective concept of the Russian Far East gas industry strategy, it is necessary to conduct an appropriate comprehensive analysis (Figure 1.1). The methodology for conducting each of its elements is described in succeeding sections of this chapter.

1.2 STRATEGIC DIAGNOSTIC METHODOLOGY FOR THE RUSSIAN FAR EAST GAS INDUSTRY

In order to choose the right long-term vector for Russian Far East gas industry development, the strategizing process should begin with a deep study of the strategizing object, namely, with strategic diagnostics [17]. At the initial stage of industrial strategizing, the main characteristics and specifics of the Russian Far East gas industry and its initial potential should

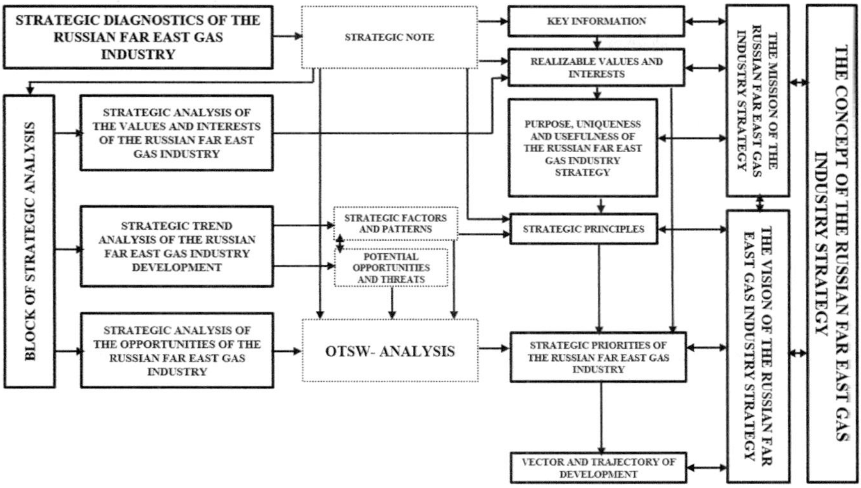

FIGURE 1.1 A conceptual scheme for the formation of the concept of the Far Eastern Federal District gas industry strategy.

Source: Compiled by the author.

be studied, and the current development trajectory should be assessed. The purpose of this primary analysis is to conduct a strategic diagnosis of the Russian Far East gas industry, which will determine the position of the strategizing object in the global and regional economic system, and form an informational basis for subsequent strategic analysis, including determining the type of potential industrial strategy (improvement strategy, innovation strategy or strategy combinations).

In accordance with the purpose of the analysis, strategic diagnostics will include a number of the following directions [18]:

1. The study of historical aspects and dynamics of the industry's development, focused on identifying the prerequisites and features of the industry's origin in the Russian Far East, including a description of the interests of different groups that helped form it.
2. Assessment of the resource base, which includes an analysis of the level of resource availability (material, financial, technical, etc.), analysis of the sustainability and availability of the resource base for the future, as well as an assessment of the human resource potential of the industry.

3. Assessment of technological potential, which involves an analysis of the level of technical equipment, scientific, and technological independence, as well as experience in implementing advanced technologies in production and their impact on Russian Far East gas industry development.
4. Analysis of the main industry indicators and the industry structure, which includes an assessment of the contribution of industry participants to its development, their ability to act as drivers for the implementation of strategic initiatives, as well as an assessment of the impact of the Russian Far East gas industry on the socio-economic development of the macro-region and the country as a whole.
5. Analysis of export potential and market positioning aimed at assessing the contribution to foreign trade and identifying key consumers of the Russian Far East gas industry.
6. Monitoring the legal and regulatory environment aimed at studying ongoing strategic documents for Russian Far East gas industry development and existing regulations, tools, and mechanisms that promote or limit the development of the industry.

1.3 STRATEGIC ANALYSIS OF THE RUSSIAN FAR EAST GAS INDUSTRY AS AN OBJECT OF INDUSTRIAL STRATEGY

This block of strategic analysis includes strategic analysis of the values and interests of the Russian Far East gas industry, strategic trend analysis of the Russian Far East gas industry development, and strategic opportunity analysis of the Russian Far Eastern Federal District (FEFD) gas industry.

1.3.1 STRATEGIC ANALYSIS OF THE VALUES AND INTERESTS OF THE RUSSIAN FAR EAST GAS INDUSTRY

It should be noted that the gas industry is not an abstract unit from the economy; it is to some extent included in a single holistic national and regional economic system, where different hierarchical levels of interaction are integrated (national, regional, industrial, corporate, public, and international) [10, 19].

Thus, in order to maintain the integrity of the general system of strategies and integrate the Russian Far East gas industry into this system, it is necessary to ensure vertical and horizontal interconnection of the gas industry with other elements within the system.

All this implies the need to analyze, systematize, and take into account all interest groups (public, national, regional, corporate, etc.) [20]. The establishment of vertical and horizontal relationships will determine the multiplicity of potential public and economic effects from the implementation of certain strategic priorities for the development of the Russian Far East gas industry [16].

It is from this point of view that it is necessary to analyze and systematize according to the main interest groups focused on the development and functioning of the Russian Far East gas industry through the prism of the socio-economic development of the region [21].

To this end, the analysis can be carried out in the context of scanning the potential sources in Table 1.1.

TABLE 1.1 Potential Sources for Interest Scanning Focused on the Development and Functioning of the Far Eastern Federal District Gas Industry (by Main Groups)

Interest Group	Potential Sources for Scanning Group Interests
National	Normative legal acts at the national level (laws, decrees, doctrines) and national-level strategies, such as: "National Security Strategy of the Russian Federation," "Economic Security Strategy of the Russian Federation for the Period Up to 2030," "Energy Strategy of the Russian Federation for the Period Up to 2035," etc.
Regional	Regulatory legal acts at the regional level (laws, decrees, doctrines), and regional development strategies, such as: "Strategies for the Socio-economic Development of the Far Eastern Federal District Subjects," "Program for Gas Supply and Gasification of Russian Regions for 2021–2025."
Corporate	Corporate documentation (strategy, annual plans, public speeches of the management team), including: The public part of Gazprom PJSC's strategy, as well as public information from PJSC "YATEK," LLC Taas-Yuryakh Neftegazodobycha, Surgutneftegaz PJSC, PJSC Rosneft.
Public	Specialized surveys, media, and personal interviews, including data from monitoring surveys on the life values of Russians (VCIOM).

Source: Compiled by the author.

1.3.2 STRATEGIC TREND ANALYSIS OF THE RUSSIAN FAR EAST GAS INDUSTRY'S DEVELOPMENT

Strategic trend analysis of the Russian Far East Gas Industry's development should be aimed at identifying strategic factors (positive and negative) [22], and patterns and trends that affect or may affect the Far Eastern Federal District gas industry in the future [11].

In addition, trend analysis is designed to provide OTSW analysis with the necessary information about existing and emerging strategic opportunities, as well as point out strategic threats.

In general, it is proposed to carry out strategic trend analysis while developing the concept of the Russian Far East Gas Industry strategy in accordance with the author's methodology, which contains some steps as in Figure 1.2 [22].

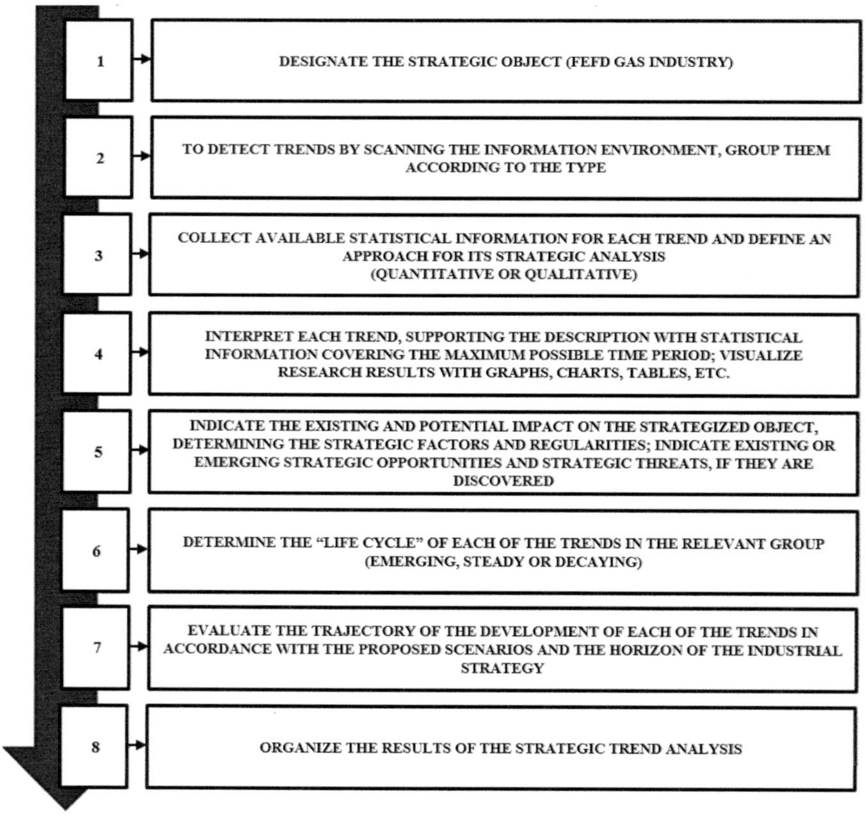

FIGURE 1.2 The main stages of strategic trend analysis in the strategizing of the Far Eastern Federal District's gas industry.

Source: Compiled by the author [22].

1.3.3 STRATEGIC ANALYSIS OF THE OPPORTUNITIES OF THE RUSSIAN FAR EAST GAS INDUSTRY

The monitoring, analysis, and justification of strategic opportunities for the development of the Russian Far East gas industry are carried out in accordance with the selective approach of OTSW analysis, which implies the algorithm in Figure 1.3 [23].

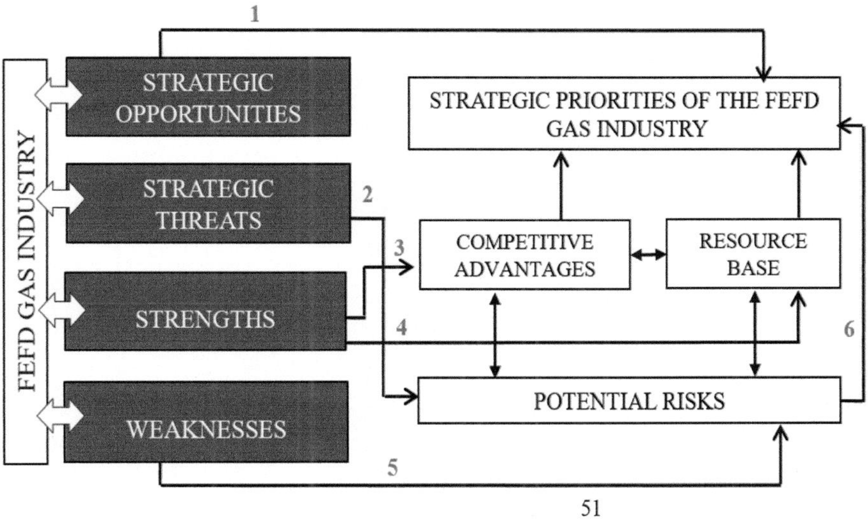

FIGURE 1.3 Conceptual diagram of the application of OTSW analysis in strategizing the Far Eastern Federal District gas industry.

Source: Compiled by the author [24].

As a first step, it is assumed that from the primary scanning of all strategic opportunities for developing the Russian Far East gas industry and determining promising strategic directions, a search and analysis of strategic threats is carried out from the position of their potential impact on implementing a single strategic opportunity within the corresponding strategic direction, or in relation to the whole strategic direction [25]. The analysis of strengths is carried out in the context of the search for competitive advantages that can ensure identified development opportunities for the Russian Far East gas industry. In turn, monitoring and taking into account weaknesses is more aimed at creating reserves or mechanisms for keeping the strategizing object on the chosen development trajectory.

Thus, based on the results of the entire comprehensive analysis, the concept of the Russian Far East gas industry strategy is formed.

KEYWORDS

- **economic effects**
- **macro-region**
- **OTSW analysis**
- **primary scanning**
- **Russian Far East gas industry strategy**
- **strategic diagnostics**
- **vertical and horizontal relationships**

REFERENCES

1. Kvint, V. L., (2016). *Strategy for the Global Market: Theory and Practical Applications*. Routledge Taylor and Francis Group.
2. Kvint, V. L., (2009). *The Global Emerging Market: Strategic Management and Economics.* Routledge.
3. Kvint, V. L., (2016). Search, and investigation of philosophical base of the theory of strategy. Interrelation of philosophical and strategic thinking. *Administrative Consulting*, (1), 15–21.
4. Kvint, V. L., (2019). *The Concept of Strategizing* (Vol. II). (Strategist' Library). IPTs SZIU RANKhiGS.
5. Kvint, V. L., (2021). *Konzepte der Strategie: Impulse für Führungskräfte*. UVK Verlag.
6. Kozyrev, A. A., (2020). Study of methodological basis of strategizing of social and economic development. *Russian Journal of Industrial Economics*, *13*(4), 434–447.
7. Ibid.
8. Kvint, V. L., & Okrepilov, V. V., (2014). Quality of life and values in national development strategies. *Herald of the Russian Academy of Sciences*, *84*(3), 188–200.
9. Dementyev, V. E., (2021). Confidence in the future as an economic development factor. *The Economic Revival of Russia*, *1*(67), 54–62.
10. Sasaev, N. I., (2022). Sectoral strategy financing: Strategic principles and efficiency. *The Economic Revival of Russia*, *4*(70), 77–87.

11. Sasaev, N. I., (2019). *Theoretical Foundations and Methodology of the Russian Gas Industry Development Strategy*. NWIM RANEPA.
12. Kvint, V. L. (2019) *The Concept of Strategizing* (Vol. I). (Strategist' Library). IPTs SZIU RANKhiGS.
13. Livchits, V. N., Mironova, I. A., & Shvetsov, A. N., (2019). Evaluating investment projects efficiency in various conditions. *Russian Journal of Industrial Economics*, *12*(1), 29–43.
14. Bakhtizin, A., Makarov, V., & Sushko, E., (2019). *Meaning of an Agent-Based Modeling in Monitoring the Implementation of the Strategy of Socio-Economic Development of the Region* (Vol. 2, No. 3). Herald of CEMI.
15. Khabriev, B. R., Bakhtizina, N. V., & Bakhtizin, A. R., (2020). Approach to an integrated assessment of the effectiveness of the development strategy of the Russian oil industry. *Russian Journal of Industrial Economics*, *13*(1), 123–131.
16. Sasaev, N., (2020). The primary assessment of the economic efficiency of strategic directions of development of gas industry in Russia. *Economics and the Mathematical Methods*, *56*(2C), 52–65.
17. Sasaev, N. I., (2021). Strategic diagnostics of the industry as a strategizing object. *Administrative Consulting*, (9), 58–68.
18. Sasaev, N. I., (2021). Strategic diagnostics at the Russian Far East gas industry. *Russian Journal of Industrial Economics*, *14*(4), 355–368.
19. Sasaev, N. I., (2021). industrial strategizing in the system of strategies (on the example of the gas industry). *Strategizing: Theory and Practice: Collection of Selected Research Articles and Proceedings of the IV International Scientific and Practical Conference* (Vol. I, pp. 72–77) Moscow Strategic Universitarium. Series "Economic and Financial Strategy," 2021; Moscow University Press.
20. Sasaev, N. I., (2021). The strategic importance of the Kuzbass trade and transport hub in sectoral and regional development. *Strategizing: Theory and Practice*, *1*(1), 99–110.
21. Sasaev, N. I., (2021). Strategizing of the Russian Far East gas industry: Systematization of main interests. *Strategizing: Theory and Practice*, *1*(2), 242–251.
22. Sasaev, N. I., (2021). Theoretical and methodological foundations of strategic trend analysis in industrial strategizing. *Models, Systems, Networks in Economics, Technology, Nature, and Society*, (4), 5–15.
23. Sasaev, N. I., (2021). Fundamental basis for the formation of a new strategizing culture. *Russian Journal of Industrial Economics*, *14*(2), 153–163.
24. Ibid.
25. Sasaev, N. I., (2022). Strategic opportunities of the Russian Far East gas industry development: Gasification, gas processing, and gas chemistry. *Strategizing: Theory and Practice*, *2*(1), 106–118.

CHAPTER 2

Strategic Diagnostics of the Russian Far East Gas Industry

2.1 HISTORICAL ASPECTS AND DYNAMICS OF THE RUSSIAN FAR EAST GAS INDUSTRY'S DEVELOPMENT

The separation of the gas industry into a separate branch of the domestic economy occurred in 1956 [1]. While analyzing the history of the gas industry in the Russian Far East, it is not possible to accurately identify the chronological stages of its origin and development due to the scale of the macro-region. Despite this, the following characteristic historical points can be noted [2].

If we consider the process of origin as forming the resource base and prerequisites as well as bearing interest in its further industrial use and building the primary infrastructure for gas production and gas transportation, then the origin stage for the Far Eastern gas industry can be correlated with the creation of the main centers of gas production.

Thus, the discovery in 1956 of the first Far Eastern gas field Ust-Vilyuiskoye in the Republic of Sakha (Yakutia) and the subsequent industrial production of natural gas there, which began a little later in the 1960s, marked the beginning of the Yakutia gas production center.

Another gas production center began with the discovery in the 1970s–1980s of gas fields in the southeastern part of the Far Eastern Federal District in the Sakhalin Region. At the same time, industrial gas production in a number of fields took place in the first decade of the twenty-first century. The Kamchatka gas production center also began operating during this approximate time.

Strategizing the Russian Gas Industry: The Far Eastern Vector. Nikita I. Sasaev (Ed)

The origin and formation of the gas industry in the Russian Far East were of particular strategic importance, since in both cases the key prerequisite was the need to address the primary issues of energy security and provide domestic consumers (households and industry) with raw energy materials [3], primarily through the network distribution of natural gas, responding to public and national interests. Nevertheless, commercial interests have also been concentrated here, implying the possibility of selling significant volumes of natural gas on the foreign market. For example, gas liquefaction and LNG exports to selected countries in the Asia-Pacific region [4].

Meanwhile, the Russian Far East gas industry is still in the initial stage of development. This is influenced and will be influenced in the long term by a number of strategic factors, among which we can mention [2]:

- Successful implementation of national and regional strategies and programs to equalize disproportionate socio-economic development in the Far East;
- Strengthening the importance of strategic proximity to the rapidly growing economies of the Asia-Pacific region (manifestation of a synergistic effect) [5];
- Implementation of a "diversification turn" in the policy of natural gas exports, with increasing gas exports to the east (including as a response to the geopolitical and energy crises in Europe) [6].

2.2 RESOURCE BASE AND HUMAN CAPACITY

There are more than 5 trillion cubic meters of natural gas reserves in the Russian Far East, including land and shelf deposits. In general, the distribution of the main natural gas reserves localized in the territory of the Far Eastern Federal District can be represented in Table 2.1.

As noted above, there are three main gas production centers: Yakutia (~65% of all gas reserves of the FEFD), Sakhalin (about one-third of the gas reserves of the FEFD), and Kamchatka (as a new gas production center) [7].

It is important to emphasize that the Republic of Sakha has a clear competitive advantage not only due to the presence of a unique oil and gas condensate field (Chayandinskoye) but also due to the content of significant amounts of valuable components in natural gas (helium, ethane, propane, butane).

Exploration work is ongoing [8], which in the long term can increase the existing reserves of gas raw materials at already-formed gas production

TABLE 2.1 The Main Fields That Form the Mineral Resource Base of the Far Eastern Federal District Gas Industry

The Republic of Sakha (Yakutia)						
Field Name	**Natural Gas**	**Helium**	**Gas Condensate**	**Ethane**	**Propane**	**Butane**
	Billion Cubic Meters	**Million Cubic Meters**	**Million Tons**			
Chayandinskoe	1,238.77	8,303.18	17.58	73.042	34.124	16.888
Srednebotuobinskoe	238.47	787.2	3.33	–	–	–
Srednevilyuiskoe	198.88	–	8.35	12.9	6.5	3
Talakan	41.33	68.9	–	–	–	–
Mastakh	30.06	–	–	–	–	–
Verkhnevilyuchanskoe	209.35	181.6	–	10.5	2.7	1.4
Tympuchikanskoye	93.8	–	–	–	–	–
Tas-Yuryakhskoe	114.04	409.1	–	–	–	–
Sobolokh-Nedzhelinsky	64.77	–	3.07	–	–	–
Middle Tyung	199.5	–	12.64	12.9	6.7	2.9
Tolon	167.4	–	8.04	–	–	–
Verkhnepeleduyskoye	14.41	–	–	–	–	–
Sakhalin Region						
Odoptu-sea (Central and Southern domes) (shelf)	101.673	–	–	–	–	–
Chaivo (shelf)	201.004	–	13.747	–	–	–
Arkutun-Dagi (shelf)	11.347	–	–	–	–	–
Lunskoye (shelf)	228.663	–	17.446	–	–	–
Piltun-Astokhskoye (shelf)	63.802	–	5.153	–	–	–
Kirinskoye (shelf)	106.812	–	13.146	–	–	–
Yuzhno-Kirinskoye (shelf)	611.739	–	97.567	–	–	–
Severo-Veninsky (shelf)	35.446	–	3.151	–	–	–
Kamchatka Krai						
Nizhnekvakchikskoe	3.908	–	0.16	–	–	–
Chukotka Autonomous Okrug						
West Lake	6.4	–	–	–	–	–

Note: Highlighted in color: developed, and white: explored.

Source: Compiled by the author based on Federal Agency for Mineral Resources materials.

centers or will allow the discovery of new deposits (including unconventional) in the remaining seven regions of the Far Eastern Federal District [9], which currently do not have their natural gas reserves.

In addition to the presence of significant natural gas reserves in the Russian Far East, the region is a leader in the extraction of other valuable minerals: diamonds (76.45% of Russian reserves); uranium (73.85% of Russian reserves); gold, silver, tin, tungsten (65.81% of Russian reserves); boron (99.68% of Russian reserves); and fluorspar (88.86% of Russian reserves) [10]. This demonstrates the possibility of long-term development of related industries that demand energy, including natural gas, and its components for gas chemistry. All this, without a doubt, determines its high natural resource potential, which is a solid foundation for industrial and regional development in the long term.

From the point of view of a personnel potential analysis, we can note the growing shortage of highly qualified labor in almost all key sectors of the economy [11, 12].

The need for the strategic development of the FEFD's human resources potential has been emphasized more than once in the works of Dr. Irina V. Novikova [13], an expert in human potential strategizing. Based on a comprehensive analysis, Novikova proposes and develops a system of strategic priorities and mechanisms for the development of labor resources in the Far Eastern Federal District. A separate promising area for the development of human resources in the web of strategic priorities is international labor cooperation [14].

The impetus for the development of the gas industry in the Russian Far East also causes a growing demand for highly qualified personnel in this area. A private solution to this problem is direct work with the younger generation in the field. In particular, as part of the long-term attraction of new human resources at the appropriate level to the high-tech production facilities of the Amur GPP, Gazprom Pererabotka Blagoveshchensk is actively working with educational institutions in the region [15].

2.3 THE FAR EASTERN GAS INDUSTRY'S TECHNOLOGICAL CAPACITY

The Russian Far East's geologic and climatic features complicate the exploration, production, and subsequent transportation of gas, which requires special and avant-garde technological solutions [16].

Particularly indicative of this difficulty is the experience of gas production from offshore fields in the Sakhalin Region [17], where specialists are faced with the most difficult task of finding and implementing innovative solutions [18]. Thus, for the development of the Kirinskoye gas condensate field, the first high-tech underwater complex was built in Russia, which makes it possible to produce hydrocarbons in the most difficult climatic conditions, including under high seismic activity conditions in the region [19]. It is noted that the onshore technological complex's facilities, which receive the produced gas mixture at the wells, are built using the dominant share of domestic technologies. Russian technologies were largely used in the design, manufacture, and installation of complex technological equipment to ensure the uninterrupted operation of the underwater complex.

At the same time, the low level of production localization and high dependence on imported equipment, such as a manifold for the above-mentioned underwater production complex [20], is one of the key reasons for holding back the development of offshore production [21].

Nevertheless, Russian design bureaus are beginning to create technologies to develop deposits in such difficult areas [22], including developing domestic underwater production complexes [23].

No less interesting in terms of technological potential is the development of the unique Chayandinskoye oil and gas condensate field, located in the Lensky district of the Republic of Sakha (Yakutia). The special thermobaric reservoir conditions and the geological structure of the field have become the determining factors when specialists of PJSC Gazprom choose the most advanced technologies for their efficient and safe development [24]. The Chayandinskoye oil and gas condensate field uses modern "small-manned technologies," which include global automation of all technological chain processes—from exploration to transportation of gas raw materials [25].

It is important to emphasize that advanced technologies have found their application not only in the process of gas production and transportation but also play a crucial role in the formation of the largest gas processing and gas chemical cluster in the Russian Far East [2]. Thus, the production facilities for liquefying natural gas (LNG), which make a significant contribution to the gas processing industry of the region, are constantly updated and introduce digital and predictive technologies that positively affect the increase in LNG production [26]. However, the Royal Dutch Shell developed the technology of gas liquefaction in large volumes [19], which still causes dependence on foreign technologies and equipment.

In addition, for the first time in the domestic practice of gas processing, it was at the Chayandinskoye oil and gas condensate field that an innovative technology for separating helium concentrate began to be applied. This technology to separate helium concentrate from gas feedstock in a two-stage hollow-fiber nanocomposite membrane plant was developed by the specialists of the "Central Design Bureau of Machine Building," "Gazprom VNIIGAZ," and "Gazprom development," [27] and has not yet been used anywhere else in the world on a scale that can be realized [28]. Without a doubt, this is a significant competitive technological advantage, which can become the basis for building an innovative development strategy [29].

The key recipient of gas feedstock components and the driver for the development of deep gas processing and gas chemistry is one of the world's largest gas processing plants—the Amur GPP [30], which also incorporates the most advanced and high-tech equipment [31].

Thus, in general, the Russian Far East has a large accumulated technological potential for the development of the gas industry, which implies a high level of technological equipment. Realizing this accumulated potential allows the creation of radically new strategic opportunities that can determine new vectors of economic development [32].

Despite this, in some areas, there is still no technological independence, which primarily affects key positions in the production cycle. This is a deterrent to the development of the Far Eastern Federal District's gas industry, especially in the context of the sanctions policy against key companies in the domestic oil and gas industry [33].

2.4 INDUSTRY PERFORMANCE AND STRUCTURE

One of the primary processes of the production cycle, which enables subsequent stages, is the extraction of minerals. In the context of strategic diagnostics, it is important to analyze a number of indicators: an analysis of the volumes of regional natural gas production in dynamics; an assessment of the production structure; and an assessment of the level of gasification [2].

Since 2010, there has been rapid growth in natural gas production in the Far Eastern Federal District. Thus, from 2010 to 2020, production volume increased by 155% and amounted to about 40.3 billion cubic meters, or 5.46% of the total natural gas production in Russia (Figure 2.1). The Sakhalin Region and the Republic of Sakha (Yakutia) remain the main production actors. Over the analyzed decade, gas production in Sakhalin increased to 33.5 billion cubic meters, or 83% of the total production of the Far Eastern Federal District in 2020. Also, a significant increase in production was observed in Yakutia, where due to the large-scale exploration of the Chayandinskoye oil and gas condensate field, production increased by more than 3.57 times compared to 2010, about 16% of the total production of the FEFD.

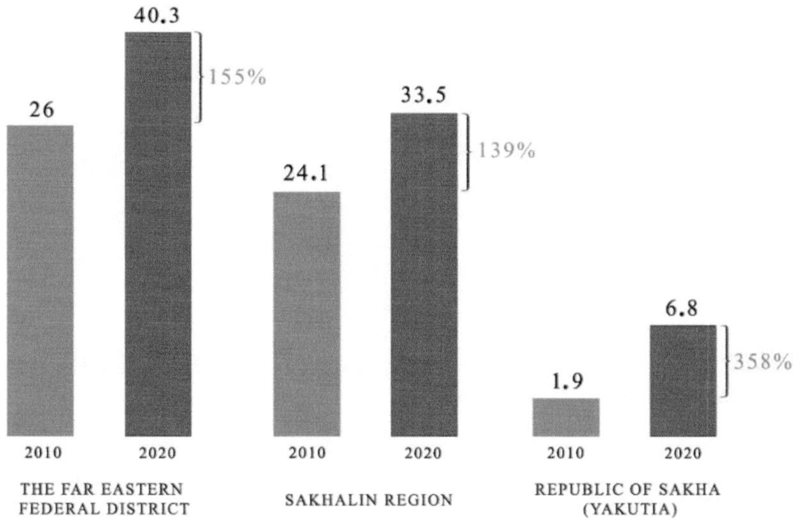

FIGURE 2.1 Dynamics of natural gas production in the Far Eastern Federal District (bcm).
Source: Compiled by the author based on the Federal State Statistics Service.

Territorial features of the distribution of natural gas reserves in the Far Eastern Federal District and natural and climatic conditions have a direct impact on the level of gasification of its constituent entities. So, out of the Far Eastern Federal District's 11 regions, only four are provided mainly with natural gas networks (Figure 2.2).

A significant increase in natural gas networks is observed in the Kamchatka Krai, where over the past 10 years the level of gasification has been raised from almost 0 to 58.9%, which became possible mainly due to the commissioning of the Sobolevo—Petropavlovsk-Kamchatsky Gas Pipeline [34].

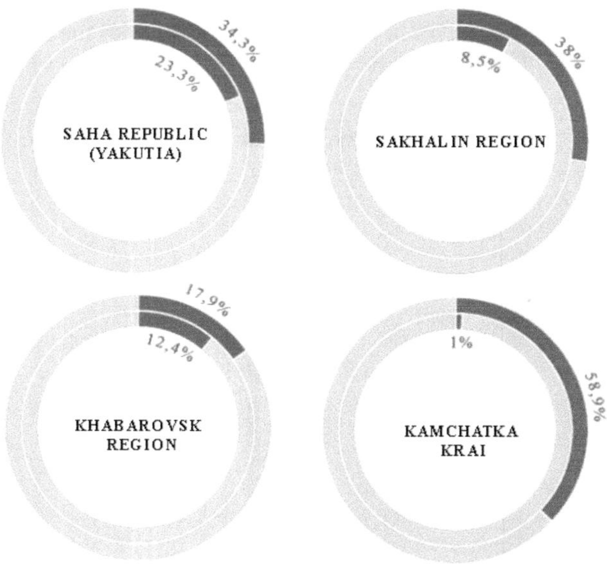

FIGURE 2.2 The gasification level of Far Eastern Federal District subjects with gas networks for 2010 and 2020 (in percentage).

Note: The inner circle indicates data for 2010, and the outer circle indicates data for 2020.

Source: Compiled by the author based on the Federal State Statistics Service and Gazprom materials.

The joint work of PJSC Gazprom and the regional authorities of the Sakhalin Region, supported by the largest investments (about 82.3 billion rubles were invested in 2014–2019 alone), made it possible to increase the gasification level of the region to 38% [35]. In turn, the increase in the Republic of Sakha (Yakutia) by 11% is associated with the active exploration of the Chayandinskoye oil and gas condensate field.

The development of gas production and gas supply will certainly become one of the driving strategic factors for stimulating the economic and social development of the Russian Far East [36, 37].

At the corporate level, the clear leaders are Gazprom PJSC, PJSC "YATEK," LLC Taas-Yuryakh Neftegazodobycha, Surgutneftegaz PJSC, PJSC Rosneft. It should be noted that PJSC Gazprom's capital investments in the Russian economy from 2017 to 2020 amounted to more than 6.3 trillion rubles [38], a significant proportion of these investments were involved in the Russian Far East in the implementation of such large-scale projects as the Power of Siberia gas pipeline, the Sakhalin-Khabarovsk-Vladivostok gas pipeline, the construction of the Chayandinskoye oil and gas condensate field, the construction of the Kirinskoye gas condensate field, the construction of the Yuzhno-Kirinskoye gas condensate field, and the implementation of regional gasification programs. The contribution of PJSC Rosneft to the GRP of Eastern Siberia and the Russian Far East is estimated at 25%, while a third of the company's investments are directed to the Far Eastern Federal District [39]. The presence of the largest oil and gas companies in the region accelerates the development of the gas industry, which in turn stimulates the growth of the regional economy [40].

2.5 EXPORT POTENTIAL AND MARKET POSITIONING

Assessing the contribution of the Russian Far East gas industry to foreign trade activities (Table 2.2), it can be noted that the Sakhalin region has remained the main actor in gas exports over the past decade, and until 2015 it was the only Russian exporter of large-scale LNG in Russia.

TABLE 2.2 Dynamics of Gas Exports of the Russian Federation and the Far Eastern Federal District

	2010		2015		2020	
	Natural Gas (billion m^3)	**LNG (million m^3)**	**Natural Gas (billion m^3)**	**LNG (million m^3)**	**Natural Gas (billion m^3)**	**LNG (million m^3)**
Russian Federation	177.8	24	185.5	21.4	202.5	68.3
Far Eastern Federal District	–	24	–	21.3	4.1	27.4
FEFD including Sakhalin Region	–	24	–	21.3	–	27.4
Share of FEFD exports in total Russian exports	0%	100%	0%	99.5%	2%	40%

Source: Compiled by the author based on the Federal Customs Service.

Since December 2019, the export of natural gas through the Power of Siberia gas pipeline to China began from the Russian Far East, so in 2020, 4.1 billion m^3 of gas was supplied to China [41]. The value of gas exports in the region's foreign trade activities in 2020 exceeded about 15.3% (more than 3.9% compared to 2010) and continues to grow rapidly, providing reliable financial and investment flows to the Far Eastern Federal District, which is backed by long-term contracts [2].

The main consumers of Russian Far East LNG are concentrated in the Asia-Pacific region (Figure 2.3), primarily Japan (51% of total LNG exports from the Far Eastern Federal District), the Republic of Korea (17%), Taiwan (16%), and China (14%).

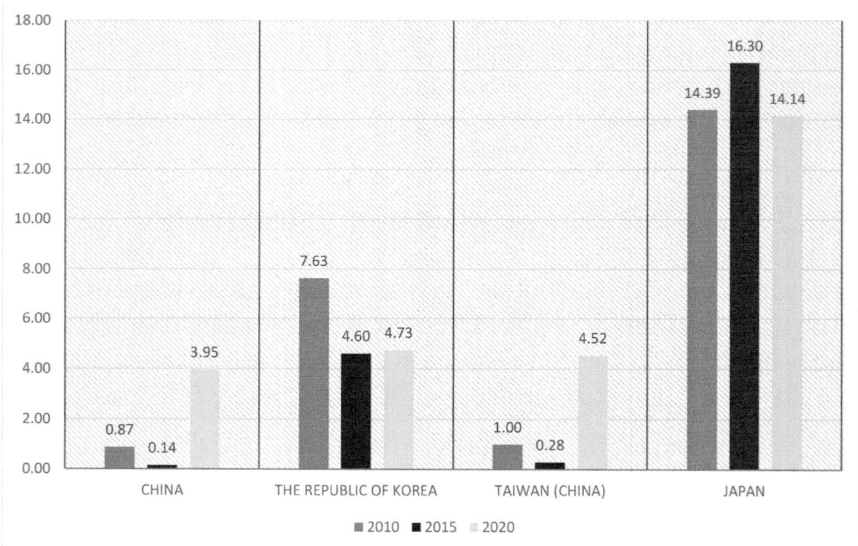

FIGURE 2.3 Country structure of Russian LNG exports from the Far Eastern Federal District (million m^3).

Source: Compiled by the author based on the Federal Customs Service.

It is worth noting that foreign recipients of Russian LNG are ready to invest in the implementation of gas projects in the Russian Far East [42].

The rapid economic development of the Russian Far East LNG consumers in the Asia-Pacific region and the long-term interest in this energy resource strengthen the export potential of the Russian Far East gas industry [6].

2.6 REGULATORY ENVIRONMENT

The regulatory and legal environment regarding the development of the gas industry in the Russian Far East is formed by a whole range of national, regional, and municipal documents of various levels (strategies, programs, plans, projects) [2], of which we will note the fundamental ones.

Since 2009, the "Strategy for the socio-economic development of the Russian Far East and the Baikal region for the period up to 2025" has been successfully implemented [43], where one of the strategic directions is the formation of a unified gas supply system in the Russian Far East and the Baikal region through the creation of a unified system of production, transportation, and providing the end consumer with gas. In addition, the export potential in the energy markets of the Asia-Pacific countries is also taken into account.

The Eastern Gas Program has implemented this strategy, which was approved by the Russian Federation's Ministry of Industry and Energy back in 2007 [44], and which is coordinated by PJSC Gazprom.

In March 2021, the "Long-term Program for the Development of Liquefied Natural Gas Production in the Russian Federation" was approved and accepted for execution, including the regulation and state support of LNG projects [45].

Since April of the same year, the approved action plan ("road map") for the implementation of a socially oriented and cost-effective gasification and gas supply system for the constituent entities of the Russian Federation has been implemented [46], which includes, among other things, the development of gas supply systems in the Russian Far East. Since June 2021, PJSC Gazprom has been implementing a large-scale Program for Gas Supply and Gasification of Russian Regions for 2021-2025, which also includes the gasification of the Far Eastern Federal District [47]. In general, the regulatory framework contributes to the implementation of national and regional interests in the Russian Far East's developing gas industry in the context of socio-economic development. Nevertheless, taking into account the methodological foundations of strategizing [48], program and project planning in the absence of a unified development strategy for the Far Eastern Federal District's gas industry in the long term can create disproportionate effects on regional development. This will undoubtedly limit the effectiveness of socio-economic development in the Russian Far East.

KEYWORDS

- **Asia-Pacific countries**
- **gas supply systems**
- **liquefied natural gas production**
- **regulatory environment**
- **Russian Federation**
- **Russian gas industry**
- **socio-economic development**

REFERENCES

1. *Chronograph of the History of the Russian Gas Industry*. http://www.mos-gaz.ru/history/industry-russia (accessed on 3 January 2023).
2. Sasaev, N. I., (2021). Strategic diagnostics at the Russian Far East gas industry. *Russian Journal of Industrial Economics*, *14*(4), 355–368.
3. Silaev, A. P., & Pershikov, A. N., (2002). New strategy for the development of the gas industry in Siberia at the turn of the XX–XXI centuries. *Bulletin of the Tomsk Polytechnic* University, *T305*(7), 144–163.
4. Sasaev, N. I., (2018). The development of large-capacity liquefied natural gas production is the strategic priority of the economic and social development of Russia. *Upravlencheskoe Konsul'tirovanie/Administrative Consulting, 8*(116), 82–95.
5. Izotov, D. A., (2020). *Economic Integration of Russia with the Asia-Pacific Countries: Problems and Prospects*. Economic Research Institute FEB RAS.
6. Sasaev, N. I., (2019). Diversification of natural gas export flows is the strategic priority for the development of the Russian gas industry. *The Economic Revival of Russia, 3*(61), 185–196.
7. *Eastern Gas Program*. Gazprom. https://neftegaz.ru/tech-library/menedzhment/141966-vostochnaya-gazovaya-programma-vgp/ (accessed on 18 January 2024).
8. *New Gas Field Discovered in Olekminsky District of Yakutia*, (2020). https://www.rosnedra.gov.ru/article/12577.html (accessed on 3 January 2023).
9. Filimonova, I. V., et al., (2019). Modern conditions and prospects for the development of gas resources in East Russia, mineral recourses of Russia. *Economics and Management*, *6*, 38–44.
10. *Information on the State and Prospects for the Use of the Mineral Resource Base of the Far Eastern Federal District*, (2021). Federal Agency for Subsoil Use. https://www.rosnedra.gov.ru/data/Fast/Files/202104/c7b093284dc7ede9f597dbe834e37688.pdf (accessed on 3 January 2023).

11. Serikov, S. G., & Ganina, T. N., (2021). Development of the Russian Far East and the Arctic: Demographic aspect. *Vestnik Universiteta*, (4), 79–86.
12. Inyutina, E. N., (2020). Activity of labor resources in the context of trends in the development of labor potential of the Far East. *Global'nyj Nauchnyj Potencial*, *3*(108), 134–138.
13. Novikova, I. V., (2020). *The Russian Far East: Strategic Development of the Workforce*. Apple Academic Press.
14. Novikova, I. V., & Yao, L., (2020). China-Russia strategic cooperation in labor development. *Administrative Consulting*, (5), 60–67.
15. *Amur GPP at the Peak of Construction: The First Gas Processing Plant in the Far East Will Become One of the Largest in the World*, (2020). Neftegaz.ru. https://magazine.neftegaz.ru/articles/pererabotka/547164-amurskiy-gpz-na-pike-stroitelstva-pervyy-gazopererabatyvayushchiy-zavod-na-dalnem-vostoke-stanet-odn (accessed on 3 January 2023).
16. Mochalov, R. A., (2015). Estimates of the complexity of oil production on the Russian shelf. *Interekspo GeoSibir [Interexpo Geo-Siberia], 3*(2), 73–78.
17. *Treasures of the Sakhalin Shelf*, (2017). Cdu.Ru. https://www.cdu.ru/tek_russia/articles/1/450 (accessed on 3 January 2023).
18. Fadeev, A., Ilyinsky, A., & Ilyin, I., (2020). *The Development of the Sea of Okhotsk Shelf: Experience in Offshore Projects Development in Difficult Climatic Conditions Using the Example of PJSC Gazprom Neft, IOP Conference Series: Earth and Environmental Science*. IOP Publishing.
19. *Sakhalin II.* Gazprom. https://www.gazprom.ru/ (accessed on 3 January 2023).
20. *Subsea Technologies on the Russian Shelf.* EnergyLand, http://m.energyland.info/index.php?action=analiticview&id=119544&offset=500&limit=10 (accessed on 3 January 2023).
21. *Development of the Russian Shelf.* Morvesti.ru. https://morvesti.ru/analitika/1691/90216/ (accessed on 18 January 2024).
22. *One of the Key Factors for the Successful Development of the Shelf is the Development of Technologies*. Sib-Science.info. http://www.sib-science.info/ru/conferences/uspeshnogo-osvoeniya-10102019 (accessed on 3 January 2023).
23. *For Sakhalin-3: Gazprom Signed an Agreement with the Almaz-Antey Concern for the Localization of Serial Production of Underwater Oil and Gas Production Complexes*, (2019). Neftegaz.ru. https://neftegaz.ru/news/Oborudovanie/194625-dlya-sakhalin-3-gazprom-podpisal-dogovor-s-kontsernom-almaz-antey-na-lokalizatsiyu-seriynogo-proizvo (accessed on 3 January 2023).
24. *Chayandinskoye Field.* https://petrodigest.ru/fields/chajandinskoe-mestorozhdenie (accessed on 18 January 2024).
25. Yamal, (2020). *"Small-manned Technologies" Helped in the Development of the Chayandinskoye Field*. Sever Press. https://sever-press.ru/news/sever-press/jamalskie-maloljudnye-tehnologii-pomogli-v-osvoenii-chajandinskogo-mestorozhdenija/ (accessed on 18 January 2024).
26. *Sakhalin Energy Shares Experience in Innovative Development of LNG Production Technologies*, (2021). Nangs.org. http://nangs.org/news/downstream/sakhalin-enerdzhi-podelilas-opytom-innovatsionnogo-razvitiya-tekhnologij-proizvodstva-spg (accessed on 3 January 2023).

27. *Amur Gas Processing Plant: Beginning of a New Era of Russian Gas Processing*, (2021). Neftegaz.ru. https://neftegaz.ru/science/pererabotka/685128-amurskiy-gazopererabatyvayushchiy-zavod-nachalo-novoy-epokhi-rossiyskoy-gazopererabotki-/ (accessed on 3 January 2023).
28. *TechnoChayanda: Efficient Technology at a Unique Field*, (2021). Neftegaz.ru. https://neftegaz.ru/science/booty/693914-tekhnochayanda-effektivnaya-tekhnologiya-na-unikalnom-mestorozhdenii-/ (accessed on 3 January 2023).
29. Kozyrev, A. A., (2015). Realization of competitive advantages of the region in the strategy of innovative development. *Central Russian Journal of Social Sciences*, *10*(6), 315–323.
30. *Amur Gas Processing Plant*. GazProm. https://www.nipigas.ru/services/our-projects/stroitelstvo-amurskogo-gpz/ (accessed on 18 January 2024).
31. Lang, M., Schmid, F., & Bauer, H., (2019). Technical concept and practical implementation of the project of the Amur gas processing plant. *GAS Industry of Russia*, *3*(781), 66–72.
32. *Gazprom and Rosatom Are Implementing a Project to Produce Hydrogen from Gas in Sakhalin*, (2021). Tass.ru. https://tass.ru/ekonomika/12297111 (accessed on 3 January 2023).
33. Ampilov, Yu. P., (2017). New challenges for the Russian petroleum industry amid sanctions and low oil prices. *Mineral'nye Resursy Rossii, Ekonomika i Upravlenie*, *2*, 38–50.
34. *Kamchatka*. Gazprom. https://www.gazprom.ru (accessed on 3 January 2023).
35. *Alexey Miller and Governor of the Sakhalin Region Valery Limarenko Discussed the Progress of the Gasification of the Region*, (2020). Gazprom. https://armtorg.ru/news/30252/ (accessed on 18 January 2024).
36. Belinskiy, A. V., (2018). Influence of the gas supply and the gas infrastructure development on economic growth of regions of the Russian Federation (econometric approach). *GAS Industry of Russia*, *S2*(770).
37. Machakhova, A. K., (2015). The gas industry is a key driver of socio-economic development in the Republic of Sakha (Yakutia) (Russia, Yakutsk). *Problems of Modern Economics*, *2*(54).
38. *Contribution to the Russian Economy*, (2020). Gazprom. https://sustainability.gazpromreport.ru/2020/3-about-gazprom/3–5-russian-economy-contribution (accessed on 3 January 2023).
39. *The Impetus for the Development of the Far East*, (2017). RBC. https://plus.rbc.ru/news/59ad84877a8aa903562aa7ea (accessed on 3 January 2023).
40. Marichev, S. G., (2021). Market attractiveness of oil and gas companies as a factor affecting the socio-economic development in regions of their business operations. *Economic Analysis: Theory and Practice*, *1*(508), 124–141.
41. *Russian Ambassador to Beijing Spoke About Gas Supplies Through the Power of Siberia*, (2021). Ria.ru. https://ria.ru/20210210/postavki-1596879079.html (accessed on 3 January 2023).
42. Han-Sol, L., (2020). The sub-national distribution of South Korean foreign direct investment in Russia: A focus on the Russian Far East. *The Tomsk State University Journal of Economics*, *52*, 280–290.

43. *On Approval of the Strategy for the Socio-economic Development of the Far East and the Baikal Region for the Period Up to 2025*. http://docs.cntd.ru (accessed on 3 January 2023).
44. *Eastern Gas Program*. Gazprom. https://neftegaz.ru/tech-library/menedzhment/141966-vostochnaya-gazovaya-programma-vgp/ (accessed on 18 January 2024).
45. *The Government Approved a Long-term Program for the Development of LNG Production*. Government.ru. http://government.ru/news/41790 (accessed on 3 January 2023).
46. *The Government Approved the "Road Map" for Increasing the Gasification of Regions*. Government.ru. http://government.ru/docs/42133 (accessed on 3 January 2023).
47. *Gazprom Will Allocate 526 Billion Rubles for the Gasification of Regions*, (2021). Bashinform. https://www.bashinform.ru/news/1605498-gazprom-vydelit-526-mlrd-rubley-na-gazifikatsiyu-regionov (accessed on 3 January 2023).
48. Darkin, S., & Kvint, V., (2016). *The Russian Far East: Strategic Priorities for Sustainable Development*, CRC Press.

CHAPTER 3

Russian Far East Gas Industry Strategizing: Systematizing Its Main Interests

3.1 THE POSITION OF THE RUSSIAN FAR EAST GAS INDUSTRY STRATEGY IN THE GENERAL SYSTEM OF STRATEGIES

Based on the methodology described above, we will initially determine the position of the Russian Far East gas industry strategy in the general system of strategies. Conceptually this can be displayed as in Figure 3.1.

It should be noted that the ideal system also implies the presence of vertical and horizontal links between the regional and industrial gas strategy of the Far Eastern Federal District with regional strategies for socio-economic development and regional and industrial gas strategies for other federal districts as well [1].

As mentioned above, the integration of the FEFD gas strategy into the general strategy system, which implies vertical and horizontal interconnection with strategies at the national level with the industrial strategies of the Far Eastern Federal District's economy, as well as with the corporate level of strategizing industrial enterprises and the personal strategies of Russian Far East residents, ensures acceptable wholeness of interests and their complementarity. It also contributes to the multiplier effect in implementing the Russian Far Eastern gas strategy on regional and industrial development and the socio-economic development of the country as a whole [2].

Strategizing the Russian Gas Industry: The Far Eastern Vector. Nikita I. Sasaev (Ed)

FIGURE 3.1 Conceptual diagram of the relationship between the regional-industrial Far Eastern Federal District gas strategy and strategies of other levels in the general system of strategies.

Source: Compiled by the author.

3.2 THE MAIN INTERESTS OF THE FAR EASTERN GAS INDUSTRY'S STRATEGIC DEVELOPMENT

The next step is to analyze the national interests localized in the Far Eastern Federal District and directly related to the strategy of the gas industry. Based on the "National Security Strategy of the Russian Federation" [3], such national interests are human development, improving the quality of life and welfare of the population, developing the economy on a new technological basis, environmental protection, environmental management, and adaptation to climate change.

National interests in the "Strategy for the Economic Security of the Russian Federation for the Period Up to 2030" are presented in an implicit form [4], but they can be determined based on the formulated national goals. Thus, among the interests in the field of ensuring the security of the Russian economy, one can note: ensuring economic growth, improving citizens' quality and standard of living, increasing economic competitiveness, and stimulating scientific and technological progress.

National interests in the energy sector are noted in the "Energy Strategy of the Russian Federation for the Period Up to 2035" [5]. Among the main ones are: assisting the fuel and energy complex in developing other economic sectors, structural diversification, ensuring the energy sector's digital transformation, and optimizing the energy structure's location, including building oil and gas mineral resource centers in the Russian Far East and elsewhere.

The public interests of Far Eastern Federal District residents generally correspond to basic values [6] and correlate with the general Russian trend [7]. The main public interests are the health, well-being, and safety of family members. Nevertheless, given region specifics [8], one of the priority interests is the financial situation and access to jobs with a decent level of wages.

The main regional interests that directly correlate with the Russian Far Eastern gas industry's strategy can be systematized as shown in Table 3.1. Note that in most strategies, there is also no explicit formulation of regional interests, however, they can be determined based on the indicated goals and priority directions.

TABLE 3.1 The Main Regional Interests Correlating with the Far Eastern Federal District Gas Industry Strategy

Far Eastern Federal District Subject	Main Regional Interests Correlated with the Far Eastern Federal District Gas Industry Strategy
The Republic of Buryatia	Development of human and industrial potentials; development of an infrastructure framework, including energy infrastructure; modernization and innovative development of economic sectors, based on the principles of environmental aspects; formation of an environmentally-oriented economy; formation of a comfortable living environment for the population and business activities.
The Republic of Sakha (Yakutia)	Affordable electricity supply; the formation of a mineral resource base that allows uninterrupted provision of population and industry needs; creation of a modern oil and gas complex with high added value; creation of a reliable gas supply system and gasification of the region in order to improve the quality of life; development of a non-resource export-oriented economy; development of small and medium business; formation of the knowledge economy and stimulation of scientific and technological progress; transition to an environmentally-oriented "green" economy.
Zabaykalsky Krai	Development of human capital; stimulation of economic growth in the main industrial areas and priorities; integration of the region into the system of international relations, primarily with Asia-Pacific countries; building interregional and international cooperation in the field of investment.

TABLE 3.1 (Continued)

Far Eastern Federal District Subject	Main Regional Interests Correlated with the Far Eastern Federal District Gas Industry Strategy
Kamchatka Krai	Formation of an efficient and balanced economy, including diversification of the regional economy; increasing the investment attractiveness of the region; creation of a developed infrastructure, including optimization of the energy infrastructure; development of the fuel and energy complex and ensuring energy efficiency; providing the population with favorable conditions for life and work.
Primorsky Krai	Improving the quality and standard of living of the population; development of the oil, gas, and petrochemical industries in the region; development of entrepreneurship, and small and medium businesses; development of the scientific and innovative sphere (including systemic support for high-tech industries); rational use of natural resources and ensuring environmental safety; ensuring energy saving and energy efficiency; development of interregional and foreign economic relations.
Khabarovsk Krai	Accumulation of human capital, comparable in basic parameters with the countries of the Asia-Pacific region, and based on increasing quality of life; creation of a comfortable space for living and economic activity; growth of competitiveness based on new industrialization, modernization, and innovation; creation and modernization of institutions that stimulate the development of an innovative, investment active economy and business environment; ensuring rational nature management and environmental safety.
Amur Region	Formation of a diversified structure of the economy with a high level of added value on a new modernized and innovative basis; advancing building infrastructure to ensure accelerated socio-economic development; improving the quality and standard of living of the population; implementation of large-scale infrastructure investment projects of federal and interregional significance, primarily the construction of a second Baikal-Amur Mainline, a gas pipeline; ensuring gasification of the region; formation of scientific and technical potential, and stimulation of scientific, technical, and innovative activity.
Magadan Region	Ensuring accelerated sustainable economic development of the region by building an efficient economy, including its diversification; introduction of technologies in production and digitalization; preservation and development of human capital; ensuring environmental safety and rational use of natural resources.

TABLE 3.1 (Continued)

Far Eastern Federal District Subject	Main Regional Interests Correlated with the Far Eastern Federal District Gas Industry Strategy
Sakhalin Region	Ensuring intensive economic growth, including through the launch of new projects for the accelerated development of the raw materials sector and the deployment of an industry services system localized in the region by industry (including the oil and gas complex); formation of an effective social sphere; accelerated development of critically important infrastructures, ensuring connectivity and efficient economic development of territories, and reducing environmental, climatic, and seismic risks (including ensuring the gasification of the region); stimulation of scientific and technological progress; development of the petrochemical industry, including toward natural gas liquefaction and its use in priority areas.

Source: Compiled by the author [9].

It is worth noting the common interest of all 11 subjects of the Far Eastern Federal District in providing natural gas to the population and industry through gasification, which is supported by the recently adopted large-scale "Program for Gas Supply and Gasification of Russian Regions for 2021–2025" [10].

Certain regions (the Republic of Sakha (Yakutia) and the Amur and Sakhalin regions) have a pronounced and well-founded interest in the expanded development of the gas industry, providing for the formation of gas processing and gas chemical clusters.

A separate study of development strategies for the economic industries of each of the subjects of the Far Eastern Federal District in order to identify interests does not have significant practical meaning, since they are to a greater extent subordinated to common regional interests and are reflected in the considered regional strategies [9]. Without a doubt, for related industries that are ready to receive natural gas as an energy source, as well as gas chemical products, this is of particular interest, as it generates competitive advantages for the formation of a competitive economy, including one that meets the environmental agenda [11].

The situation is similar at the corporate level. For industrial enterprises, which are the main actors in the implementation of regional and industrial strategies, obtaining a highly efficient source of energy and relatively cheap domestic gas chemistry products can expand their production capabilities, as well as increase the competitiveness of their products in the interregional and international markets.

Separately, it is worth noting the interests of enterprises in the oil and gas sector. For example, oil and gas corporations localized in the Sakhalin Region are interested in providing access to cutting-edge technologies in the field of exploration and production of Sakhalin shelf resources, improving the efficiency of training labor resources and human resources on the basis of educational institutions in the region, as well as creating conditions for exploring and building a regional mineral resource base [12].

In addition, while analyzing the strategy of PJSC Gazprom, it is possible to determine some of its corporate interests, which are focused on the gas industry of the Russian Far East. These include strengthening the status of a lead supplier of efficient and environmentally friendly fossil fuels, both in the domestic and foreign markets, as well as diversifying sales markets [13].

China, South Korea, Japan, and other Asia-Pacific countries, which are long-term consumers of Far Eastern natural gas and gas chemistry products in the foreign market, are also interested in the development and successful functioning of the Russian Far East gas industry [14, 15].

KEYWORDS

- **Asia-Pacific countries**
- **gas chemistry**
- **long-term consumers**
- **natural gas**
- **PJSC Gazprom**
- **Russian Far East gas industry**
- **Sakhalin shelf resources**

REFERENCES

1. Sasaev, N. I., (2021). Strategizing of the Russian Far East gas industry: Systematization of main interests. *Strategizing: Theory and Practice, 1*(2), 242–251.

2. Sasaev, (2021). *Strategizing of the Russian Far East Gas Industry: Systematization of Main Interests.*
3. *Russian Federation Presidential Decree of July 2, No. 400 "On the National Security Strategy of the Russian Federation."* Kremlin.ru. http://www.kremlin.ru/acts/bank/47046 (accessed on 3 January 2023).
4. *Russian Federation Presidential Decree of May 13, 2017 No. 208 "On the Strategy for the Economic Security of the Russian Federation for the Period Up to 2030."* Kremlin.ru. http://kremlin.ru/acts/bank/41921 (accessed on 3 January 2023).
5. *Decree of the Government of the Russian Federation of 09.06.2020 N 1523-r "On Approval of the Energy Strategy of the Russian Federation for the Period Up to 2035."* Minenergo.gov.ru, https://minenergo.gov.ru/node/1026 (accessed on 3 January 2023).
6. Maslow, A. H., (1943). A Theory of Human Motivation. *Psychological Review*, *50*(4), 370.
7. *Data From a Monitoring Survey on the Life Values of Russians for 2020 by VCIOM*, (2020). https://wciom.ru/analytical-reviews/analiticheskii-obzor/zdorove-bezopasnost-semya-i-rabota (accessed on 3 January 2023).
8. Novikova, *The Russian Far East: Strategic Development of the Workforce.*
9. Sasaev, *Strategizing of the Russian Far East Gas Industry: Systematization of Main Interests.*
10. *Gazprom Will Allocate 526 billion Rubles for the Gasification of Regions.* https://www.bashinform.ru/news/1605498-gazprom-vydelit-526-mlrd-rubley-na-gazifikatsiyu-regionov (accessed on 3 January 2023).
11. Sasaev, N. I., (2019). *Theoretical Foundations and Methodology of the Russian Gas Industry Development Strategy.* NWIM RANEPA.
12. *On the Approval of the Strategy for the Socio-economic Development of the Sakhalin Region for the Period Up to 2035.* https://docs.cntd.ru (accessed on 3 January 2023).
13. Strategy, PJSC Gazprom. https://www.interfax.ru/business/656140 accessed on 18 January 2024).
14. Han-Sol, L. *The Sub-national Distribution of South Korean Foreign Direct Investment in Russia: A Focus on the Russian Far East.*
15. Ko, J., (2019). The LNG market in Northeast Asia and recommendations for Russian LNG exports. *Russian Foreign Economic Journal, 9.*

CHAPTER 4

Strategic Trend Analysis of the Russian Far East Gas Industry Development

4.1 GLOBAL TRENDS

4.1.1 CLIMATE CHANGE

The Intergovernmental Panel on Climate Change (IPCC) notes an increase in the global trend associated with a significant change in climatic conditions, which has a number of negative consequences [1]. Experts assume that as a result of global warming, the average temperature will increase by more than 1.5°C in the period from 2030 to 2050. It should be noted that the reduction of economic and industrial activity associated with COVID-19, of course, caused a slowdown in this trend, however, according to the World Meteorological Organization, this effect is only short-term [2].

The strategic factor that has a direct impact on climate change is negative environmental changes, most often caused by anthropogenic impact [3]. For example, from 1980 to 2019, global carbon dioxide emissions increased by more than 1.83 times, while Asia-Pacific countries contributed the most to the change, providing more than 87% of growth and becoming the leader in carbon dioxide emissions (Table 4.1) [4]. According to British Petroleum experts, while maintaining the current trend of annual increases in emissions throughout a number of world regions (baseline scenario), in the mid-2020s a peak is expected, after which a slow decline in global carbon dioxide emissions is expected until 2050 [5], which implies a fairly stable nature of this trend in the long term.

Strategizing the Russian Gas Industry: The Far Eastern Vector. Nikita I. Sasaev (Ed)

TABLE 4.1 The Volume of Carbon Dioxide Emissions in the Global and Regional Context (Million Tons)

	1980	1990	2000	2010	2019	2020
Total North America	5399.2	5698.5	6646.7	6499.9	6067.1	5348.1
Total S. & Cent. America	628.1	675.2	932.1	1198.5	1274.5	1157.7
Total Europe	4810.6	5466.3	4794.7	4677.5	4091.3	3596.8
Total CIS	3306.0	2875.4	1814.4	1980.9	2165.6	2039.5
Total Middle East	482.0	724.0	1085.3	1765.6	2190.2	2110.1
Total Africa	517.8	735.1	864.5	1171.6	1364.5	1254.0
Total Asia Pacific	3575.6	5374.4	7710.2	13997.5	17203.3	16778.0
Total World	18719.3	21548.9	23847.9	31291.4	34356.6	32284.1

Source: Compiled by the author based on the BP Statistical Review of World Energy (2021).

In order to reverse this trend in global climate change by reducing pollutant emissions, various regulatory programs and measures are being adopted and implemented at different levels, including the Paris Agreement on Combating Climate Change, which was adopted in 2015 [6]. At the national level, strategic initiatives are being developed to transform the environmental sphere with a transition to the principles of a "green" economy [7].

4.1.2 ENERGY MARKET TRANSFORMATION

The formation of a global market space that favors the development of international trade in energy resources, and the emerging need to fulfill obligations to transform national energy systems in the context of combating pollutant emissions, led to structural changes in the energy market (Table 4.2) [8].

TABLE 4.2 Changing Energy Balances Changing in the Global and Regional Context (in percentage).

	North America			S. & Cent. America		
	1980	2019	2020	1980	2019	2020
Oil	46%	39%	37%	65%	43%	42%
Gas	25%	33%	35%	12%	22%	21%
Coal	19%	11%	9%	4%	5%	6%
Nuclear	3%	7%	8%	0%	1%	1%
Hydroelectricity	6%	5%	6%	18%	23%	23%

TABLE 4.2 (Continued)

	North America			S. & Cent. America		
	1980	**2019**	**2020**	**1980**	**2019**	**2020**
Renewables	0%	4%	5%	0%	6%	7%
	Middle East			**Africa**		
	1980	2019	2020	1980	2019	2020
Oil	75%	45%	43%	49%	42%	39%
Gas	22%	52%	55%	11%	28%	30%
Coal	1%	1%	1%	32%	22%	22%
Nuclear	0%	0%	0%	0%	1%	1%
Hydroelectricity	2%	1%	1%	8%	6%	7%
Renewables	0%	0%	0%	0%	2%	2%
	Europe			**CIS**		
	1980	**2019**	**2020**	**1980**	**2019**	**2020**
Oil	47%	37%	34%	37%	22%	22%
Gas	14%	24%	26%	28%	53%	52%
Coal	29%	13%	12%	29%	14%	14%
Nuclear	3%	10%	10%	2%	5%	5%
Hydroelectricity	6%	7%	8%	4%	6%	6%
Renewables	0%	9%	11%	0%	0%	0%
	Asia Pacific			**World**		
	1980	**2019**	**2020**	**1980**	**2019**	**2020**
Oil	45%	28%	26%	46%	33%	31%
Gas	5%	12%	12%	18%	24%	25%
Coal	42%	48%	48%	27%	27%	27%
Nuclear	2%	2%	2%	3%	4%	4%
Hydroelectricity	6%	6%	6%	6%	7%	7%
Renewables	0%	4%	5%	0%	4%	5%

Source: Compiled by the author based on the BP Statistical Review of World Energy (2021).

One of the strategic factors of transformation was the shift away from "dirty" energy sources. From 1980 to 2019, the share of oil used in the global energy balance has significantly decreased. In turn, natural gas and alternative sources have become more frequently used energy sources [8].

It should be noted that in other regions in addition to the Asia-Pacific, there is a tendency to increase "clean" energy sources in national energy balances. At the same time, according to expert estimates, it is natural gas and alternative energy sources that will become the dominant force in the context of reducing emissions into the atmosphere from the energy sector [5]. Thus, already in 43 countries of the world, natural gas occupies a significant place in the national energy balance, and in 17 countries the dominant place.

The confirmed intentions of national governments to improve the global environmental situation make it possible to assess this global energy trend as sustainable in the long term.

The proximity of the Russian Far East to growing energy markets opens up strategic opportunities for the long-term development of the gas industry in the region.

4.1.3 FORMATION OF THE GLOBAL NATURAL GAS MARKET

For a long time, the system of interregional natural gas trade was dominated by pipeline trade. Meanwhile, since the 2000s, the share of trade in liquefied natural gas began to gradually increase (Figure 4.1). Thus, from 2000 to 2019, the shares of pipeline and liquefied natural gas in interregional trade leveled off, and at the end of this period, they were almost equal (51.1% and 48.9%, respectively). Interestingly, the LNG trade proved to be more resilient than the pipeline gas trade during the COVID-19 pandemic, which in the short term brought it to a leading position.

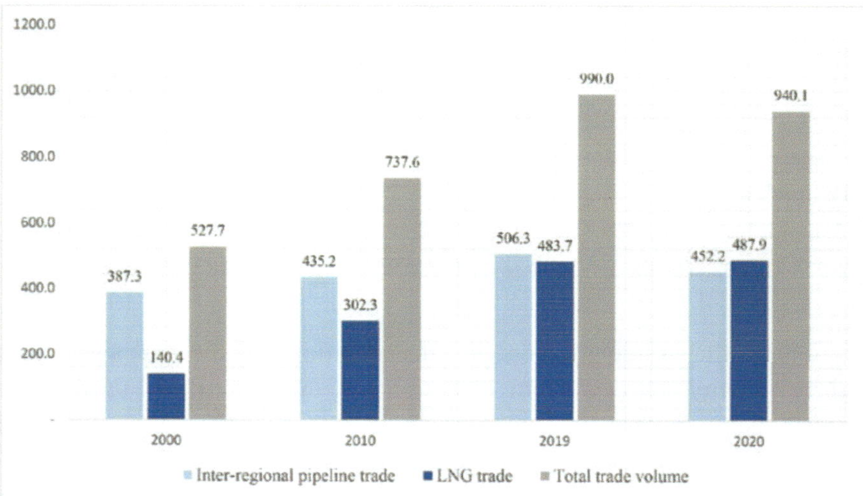

FIGURE 4.1 Inter-regional natural gas and LNG trade (bcm).

Source: Compiled by the author based on the BP Statistical Review of World Energy (2021).

The main gas importers for 2020 were East and South Asian countries and Asia-Pacific Region countries (42% of total natural gas imports). More than 72% of LNG imports were also provided by Asian countries, of which about 30% of LNG imports came from China. Long-term forecasts regarding the development of LNG trade in the world market estimate its potential growth at more than 2.6 times by 2030 [9].

It is indeed thanks to the development of world trade in liquefied natural gas that the global natural gas market is being formed [10], which can strengthen the positions of international organizations (e.g., The Gas Exporting Countries Forum) to develop mutual understanding between the parties involved in the relevant transactions, as well as to regulate the world market natural gas.

This global long-term energy trend has a direct positive impact on the development of the Far Eastern Federal District's gas industry, which has production capacities for the liquefaction of natural gas in large-scale volumes [8].

4.1.4 THE SPREAD OF COVID-19

The outbreak of a new coronavirus infection in late 2019 and early 2020, initially localized in the city of Wuhan (Hubei Province, China), spread across the whole world in just three months [11]. From January 2020 to November 2021, the number of detected diseases exceeded 255 million people, of which more than 5.1 million deaths were recorded [12]. On the one hand, the impact of the spread of the coronavirus infection significantly affected a decline in business activity; on the other hand, it intensified structural changes in the economy and public life, including accelerating the processes of digitalization [8]. Due to the association with seasonal fluctuations that create new waves of coronavirus infection, and low rates of vaccination (at the time of the trend analysis, only slightly more than 41% of the world population was fully vaccinated), the existing forecasts are not able to give an unambiguous answer on the scenario of further spread of COVID-19 in the medium and long term [13].

Such a negative strategic factor as COVID-19 has and, most likely, will continue to have a negative impact on socio-economic development and business activity on a global scale, which may also affect the development of the gas industry in the Russian Far East, acting as one of the limiting factors in energy consumption, including natural gas.

4.1.5 TECHNOLOGICAL TRANSFORMATION AND DIGITALIZATION

Another technological transformation—the transition to Industry 4.0—has led to the emergence of a global trend associated with the massive and widespread introduction of a whole range of digital technologies: the industrial internet of things, augmented and virtual reality, digital twins, big data processing, neurotechnologies, and artificial intelligence, digital technology, smart cities, and more [14].

Implemented digital technologies are gradually becoming one of the strategic factors that ensure economic growth [15]. So, if in 2015 the share of the digital economy in global GDP was about 22.5% [16], then by 2020 the contribution of the digital economy to global GDP is estimated at 27% with a potential growth of up to 50% by the end of 2025 [17].

The implementation of digital technologies in the economy and industries is also one of Russia's strategic tasks, the solution of which can stimulate the long-term socio-economic development of the country as a whole and its regions, including the Far Eastern Federal District [18].

4.2 INTERNATIONAL REGIONAL TRENDS

4.2.1 INDUSTRIAL CENTER DISPLACEMENT

The high rates of economic growth in developing countries over a long period, covering the last three decades, are associated with a surge in industrial development. This formed a global trend to increase production capacities in such countries and became one of the significant reasons for the shift of industrial centers from one region of the world to another [19].

For example, the contribution of East Asia and the Pacific region to the global manufacturing output increased by more than 15% from 2004 to 2020 and is 46%, while the contribution of Europe and Central Asia during the same period decreased by 11% and amounted to 23% of the total global manufacturing output (Figure 4.2) [8]. The main actor in this transformation process by country is China (29% in 2020). Low wages and proximity to large consumer markets remain among the key strategic factors that can support this trend in the long term [20].

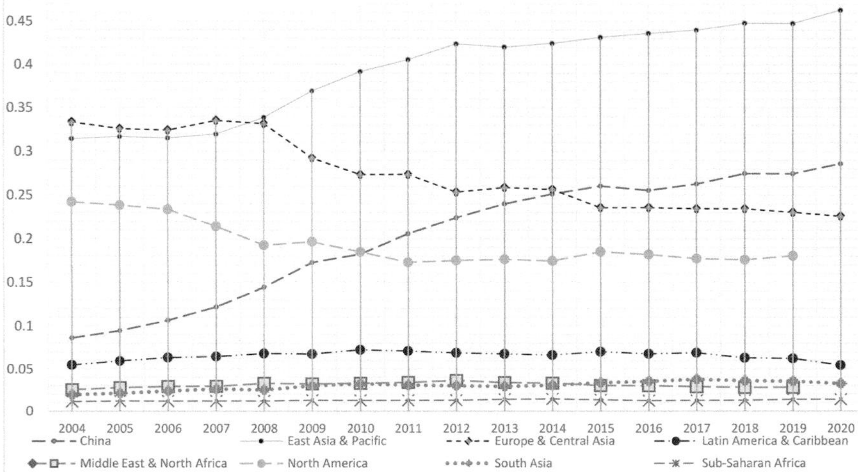

FIGURE 4.2 Contribution of regions to the global manufacturing output (in percentage).

Note: No data is available for North America, the Middle East, and North Africa for 2020.

Source: Compiled by the author based on the World Bank Open Data.

For the Far Eastern Federal District and its gas industry, respectively, this global industrial trend opens up a number of strategic opportunities, since it implies a mandatory increase in energy consumption in response to an increase in the production capacity of the manufacturing industry. It is worth emphasizing that the demand for energy resources from the industry is the second most important in the sectoral context of global energy demand (which covers about a third of the total demand). ExxonMobil estimates suggest that this proportion will remain until 2040 [21].

4.2.2 GROWING DEMAND FOR POLYMERS

Accelerated industrial development in a number of world regions forms another significant trend, primarily related to the oil and gas industry, which is namely the growth in demand for polymers. According to forecasts from 2019 to 2030, the polymer market will have an annual growth of 5.1%, the market volume by the end of the period will increase by more than 1.57 times and amount to $838.5 billion [22], while in the countries of the Asia-Pacific region, the market will grow faster, and China will account for about 32% of the total market.

It is noted that it is the oil and gas chemistry that can meet these growing needs in the long term [23]. The growth in demand for polymers can become one of the strategic factors ensuring the growth of demand for natural gas in the region, which opens up a strategic opportunity for the gas industry of the Russian Far East [24].

4.2.3 UNCONVENTIONAL GAS SOURCES

In the last two decades, in some regions of the world, special attention has been paid to the extraction of natural gas from unconventional sources, primarily from shale. The most popular shale gas production through hydraulic fracturing technology has been utilized in the United States. For the period 2007–2019, shale gas production by US companies increased almost 20 times [25].

The potential for shale gas production is also available in a number of Asia-Pacific countries. Back in 2019, shale gas reserves in the Chinese province of Sichuan were estimated at 31.6 trillion cubic meters of gas [19]. In accordance with China's long-term plans, it is planned to increase gas production from shale by 2030 to 80–100 billion cubic meters. However, according to experts, the potential production volume will not exceed 50 billion cubic meters per year [26].

Unfortunately, a number of negative consequences associated with the use of hydraulic fracturing technology do not allow us to speak about the sustainability of this energy trend in the long term, especially in the face of environmental degradation.

In general, this trend may have a negative impact on the development of the gas industry in the Russian Far East, primarily because if China can increase its gas production, then it will be able to meet part of its needs while simultaneously reducing imports of energy resources [8].

4.3 GENERAL NATIONAL TRENDS

4.3.1 IMPORT SUBSTITUTION OF EQUIPMENT IN THE FUEL AND ENERGY COMPLEX

In response to the 2014 introduction of sectoral sanctions against key partners of the Russian fuel and energy complex, including those providing for the restriction of transferring foreign technologies and equipment by Russian energy companies, the Russian Ministry of Energy, in cooperation with the Ministry of Industry and Trade, began active work on import substitution in this area [27]. Thus only from 2015 to 2020, the share of imported oil and gas equipment decreased from 60% to 43% [28].

Of particular note is the reduction in dependence on imports for the necessary equipment to produce liquefied natural gas and implement offshore projects to 67.8% (in 2015, the share was 80 and 85%, respectively) [29]. At the same time, national support for the domestic oil and gas engineering industry will continue, according to estimates until 2024, and more than 30 billion rubles will be directed to this direction alone, which confirms the stability of this industrial trend at least in the medium term.

4.4 INDUSTRIAL NATIONAL TRENDS

4.4.1 DIGITAL TECHNOLOGIES IN THE FUEL AND ENERGY COMPLEX

This national technological trend was formed in Russia back in the early 2000s, with the active introduction of dispatch control systems, data collection and analysis systems (SCADA), digital technologies such as "smart fields," and other technologies [19].

In the past few years, there has been an increase in this trend, primarily due to the 2019 formation, on the initiative of the Ministry of Energy together with the fuel and energy companies, of the departmental project "Digital Energy" [30]. Thus, the working group "Digital Transformation of the Oil and Gas Industry," which became the central link within this departmental project and included 28 participants (representatives of ministries, Russian oil and gas companies, and interested departments), developed measures for digital transformation at the beginning of 2020, the implementation of which can provide oil and gas enterprises with an annual savings of 200–280 billion rubles by 2035. Particular attention is paid to the issues of import substitution of software, the development of unmanned technologies, as well as technologies for ensuring state control and other services.

The availability of domestic equipment in the oil and gas sector and the introduction of digital technologies are some of the most important strategic factors contributing to the long-term development of the gas industry in the Russian Far East, including providing the opportunity to extract hard-to-recover natural gas reserves in difficult climatic and geographical conditions [8].

4.4.2 *IMPLEMENTING A DIVERSIFICATION REVERSAL*

The European energy market has been a key one throughout the history of the Russian gas industry. Nevertheless, given the instability associated with the manifestation of energy, economic, and political crises in Europe, and on the other hand, the preservation of high rates of economic development in the Asia-Pacific countries despite the global crises, there is a tendency to increase the volume of exports toward the east [31]. Due to the launch of natural gas liquefaction facilities in the Russian Far East in 2009 (implementation of the Sakhalin-2 project) and LNG exports to a number of countries in the Asia-Pacific region, the share of gas exports to these countries in total volume increased from zero to 11% for 2020 (Figure 4.3).

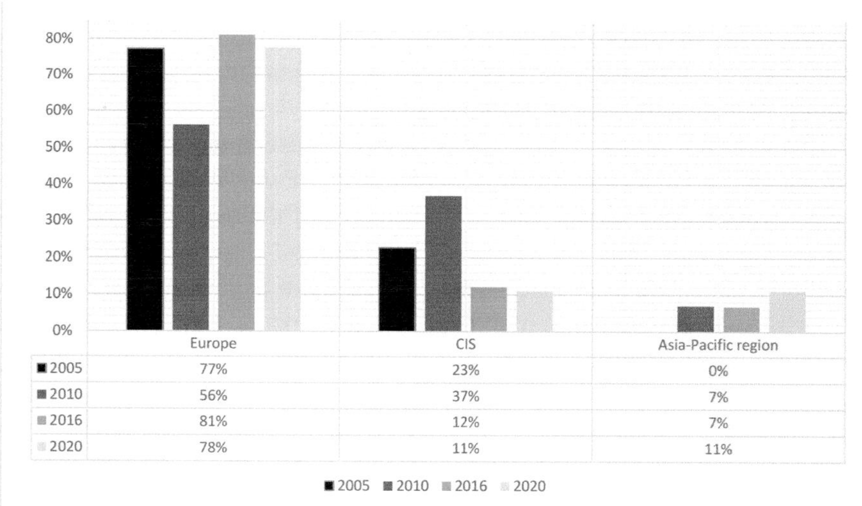

FIGURE 4.3 Distribution of natural gas and LNG exports by the main recipient regions (in percentage of the total volume).

Source: Compiled by the author based on the BP Statistical Review of World Energy (2021).

At the same time, this industrial trend in the national context can be characterized as an emerging one, the long-term view and scale of which is confirmed by the implementation of a number of major gas projects, including the Power of Siberia gas pipeline project, through which 4.1 billion cubic meters of natural gas was delivered to China in 2020 [32].

Without a doubt, the implementation of a diversification turn opens up a number of strategic opportunities for the development of the Russian Far East gas industry.

4.5 THE RUSSIAN FAR EAST REGIONAL TRENDS

4.5.1 POPULATION DECLINE IN THE REGION

In the Russian Far East, a long-term trend of population decline continues. From 2011 to 2020, the total population of the Far Eastern Federal District decreased by more than 1,56,000 people. This reduction occurred in almost all FEFD subjects with the exception of the Republic of Buryatia and the Republic of Sakha (Yakutia) (Table 4.3) [8].

TABLE 4.3 Population by the Regions of the Far Eastern Federal District (1,000 People)

FEFD Subjects	2011	2015	2020	Change from 2011 to 2020
The Republic of Buryatia	972.2	978.5	985.9	101.4%
The Republic of Sakha (Yakutia)	958.3	956.9	972.0	101.4%
Zabaykalsky Krai	1106.2	1087.5	1059.7	95.8%
Kamchatka Krai	321.7	317.3	313.0	97.3%
Primorsky Krai	1953.4	1933.3	1933.3	99.0%
Khabarovsk Krai	1342.9	1338.3	1315.6	98.0%
Amur Region	828.7	809.9	790.0	95.3%
Magadan Region	156.5	148.1	140.1	89.5%
Sakhalin Region	496.7	488.4	488.3	98.3%
Jewish Autonomous Region	176.3	168.4	158.3	89.8%
Chukotka Autonomous Region	50.3	50.5	50.3	99.9%
Total Population	8363.2	8277.0	8206.6	98.1%

Source: Compiled by the author based on the Federal State Statistics Service.

One of the strategic factors negatively affecting the population in the region is the outflow of the population, most often associated with insufficient wages and a lack of jobs [33, 34]. However, a number of measures are being taken to reverse this trend in the medium term [35].

Achieving demographic stability in the region is of high importance for the long-term development of the gas industry in the Russian Far East, as households are one of the key energy consumers.

4.5.2 INDUSTRIAL STABILITY

Analyzing the dynamics of production in the Russian Far East from 2015 to 2019, we can find a generally positive trend in the development of industrial, manufacturing, and mining industries (Table 4.4) [8].

We also note that production indicators in 2020 decreased due to restrictions caused by the COVID-19 pandemic, however, the decrease was of a short-term nature and, according to experts, recovery and return to the original trajectory began already in 2021 [36].

Industry is a key energy consumer, which is why the growth of industrial production is also an important strategic factor for the development of the Russian Far Eastern gas industry.

One of the strategic factors that can ensure demographic stability and industrial development in the region is the development of infrastructure [37]. According to estimates, about 2,000 infrastructure projects are already being implemented, and there is a positive trend in the annual growth of budget investments in the infrastructure of the entire Russian Far East and its subjects (Figure 4.4) [8].

Significant volumes of infrastructure investments are coming to the Sakhalin Region, the Republic of Sakha (Yakutia), the Khabarovsk Krai, the Republic of Buryatia, and the Amur Region. Foreign investment is another strategic factor, so since 2018 the number of investment projects with Chinese participation, including infrastructure projects, has more than doubled and amounted to 59 in 2021 [39].

4.6 CORPORATE TRENDS

4.6.1 TRANSITION OF OIL AND GAS COMPANIES TO TECHNOLOGICAL INDEPENDENCE

One of the most important trends at the corporate level, related to technological aspects, was formed as a response to the sanctions policy

TABLE 4.4 Production Indices for Certain Types of Economic Activities by Regions of the Far Eastern Federal District (in Percentage to the Previous Year)

Economic Activity	Year	Russian Federation	Far Eastern Federal District	The Republic of Buryatia	The Republic of Sakha (Yakutia)	Zabaykalsky Krai	Kamchatka Krai	Primorsky Krai	Khabarovsk Krai	Amur Region	Magadan Region	Sakhalin Region	Jewish Autonomous Region	Chukotka Autonomous Region
Industrial Production	2015	100.2	104.4	100.9	105.8	98.8	103.4	90.5	99.4	90.7	106.4	111.9	81.9	102.6
	2016	101.8	103.4	88.9	100.8	104.8	110.1	106.0	108.4	96.0	101.9	105.9	99.5	91.7
	2017	103.7	103.1	101.3	102.5	103.7	105.7	118.7	109.1	105.3	107.7	99.9	160.4	90.2
	2018	103.5	105.4	102.4	107.6	103.8	112.8	96.4	100.3	97.6	109.6	106.4	114.9	100.4
	2019	103.4	106.6	111.6	111.3	105.6	95.5	118.2	102.5	109.9	112.6	102.8	102.6	105.8
	2020	97.9	96.0	113.2	95.3	99.4	94.3	80.5	100.5	95.7	105.7	96.9	102.4	101.0
Extraction of Mineral Resources	2015	101.3	107.4	95.6	106.7	104.3	109.7	82.4	98.8	90.6	108.5	112.5	133.0	106.8
	2016	102.6	102.8	101.3	100.7	108.1	150.1	83.7	97.7	88.8	100.9	105.5	193.7	89.6
	2017	101.9	102.1	106.9	102.7	108.1	97.9	96.8	118.2	113.8	109.2	100.0	542.6	86.3
	2018	103.8	107.0	108.6	108.4	106.4	92.9	119.2	103.2	90.2	110.7	107.0	141.5	100.2
	2019	103.4	106.8	127.0	112.3	107.9	89.0	115.8	102.8	115.9	113.6	102.4	114.7	104.0
	2020	93.4	96.5	118.2	94.8	99.8	104.5	95.3	101.3	91.1	103.5	96.0	108.3	100.2
Manufacturing	2015	99.9	95.3	103.0	94.8	99.3	104.1	86.1	98.7	89.7	103.3	102.4	72.6	42.3
	2016	101.1	107.4	83.3	101.5	92.4	104.7	115.3	115.7	89.9	115.7	115.4	89.3	102.5
	2017	105.7	109.9	97.0	103.4	88.3	111.0	127.6	107.7	104.6	106.1	97.3	119.6	119.0
	2018	103.6	100.7	102.6	96.9	95.5	120.2	92.8	97.9	104.4	102.3	94.8	95.7	114.3
	2019	103.6	109.3	111.9	110.5	106.3	94.9	124.9	103.8	101.5	128.3	111.9	90.3	251.8
	2020	101.4	91.9	116.2	97.9	94.2	91.5	75.8	102.2	94.3	174.0	112.0	90.5	79.0

Source: Compiled by the author based on the Federal State Statistics Service.

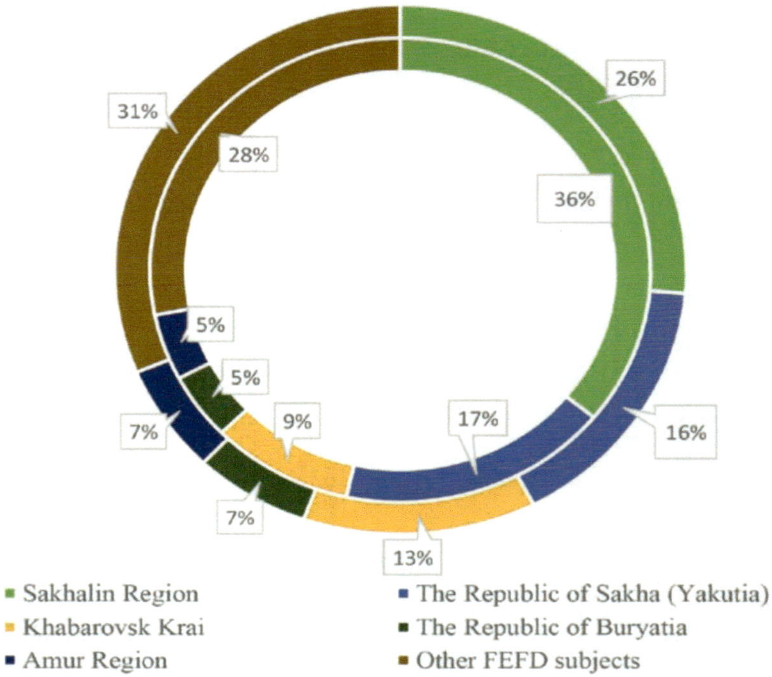

FIGURE 4.4 Distribution of budget investments in the Far Eastern Federal District infrastructure for 2015 and 2020 (in Percentage).

Note: Inner circle: data for 2015; and outer circle: data for 2020.

Source: Compiled by the author based on the analytical review InfraOne Research's "Investments in Infrastructure: The Far East" (2021) [38].

noted above in relation to Russian oil and gas companies and their partners.

This situation significantly limited the development of the oil and gas sector, reducing access to key technologies and equipment. In this regard, in order to eliminate technological dependence, a number of oil and gas companies have strengthened their interaction with domestic enterprises in the development of Russian technologies and equipment.

Since 2017, NOVATEK has been actively cooperating with "Atomenergomash," "HMS Group," "Severgroup," and "Tyazhmash." Gazprom implements a number of strategic projects jointly with "Rosatom," "Roscosmos," "Rostec," and "Severgroup" [40]. During the period of technological import substitution, NOVATEK has developed a unique Russian technology for liquefying natural gas and has already put into operation at full design capacity one of the Yamal LNG lines built on its basis [41]. “Gazprom” received a unique technology in the world for the extraction of helium concentrate from gas raw materials on a large scale [42]; in the near future, the company plans to obtain domestic technologies for the underwater production of natural gas and oil, in connection with which an agreement was reached with the Almaz-Antey Corporation [43].

The digital transformation of the oil and gas sector, which is based on Russian software, is also not sidelined. For example, Rosneft plans to completely switch to its developments and software in the field of exploration and production of hydrocarbons by 2025 [30].

This corporate technological trend will have a positive impact on the Russian Far East gas industry since it is a high-tech oil and gas company that can act as a driver for its long-term development and reliable operation [44].

KEYWORDS

- **climate change**
- **COVID-19**
- **digitalization**
- **energy complex**
- **international regional trends**
- **polymers**
- **unconventional gas sources**

REFERENCES

1. *Global Warming of 1.5°C*, (2018). Special Report, IPCC. https://www.ipcc.ch/sr15 (accessed on 3 January 2023).
2. *Climate Change and Impacts Accelerate.* https://public.wmo.int/en/media/press-release/climate-change-and-impacts-accelerate (accessed on 3 January 2023).

3. Bondarenko, L. V., Maslova, O. V., Belkina, A. V., & Sukhareva, K. V., (2018). Global climate changing and its after-effects. *Vestnik of the Plekhanov Russian University of Economics*, (2), 84–93.
4. Sasaev, N. I., (2022). Strategic analysis of trends in the development of the Russian Far East gas industry. *Economic Analysis: Theory and Practice*, *21*(3), 416–441.
5. *Energy Outlook: 2020 Edition.* BP. https://www.bp.com/content/dam/bp/business-sites/en/global/corporate/pdfs/energy-economics/energy-outlook/bp-energy-outlook-2020.pdf (accessed on 3 January 2023).
6. Paris Agreement, UNFCCC. http://unfccc.int/resource/docs/2015/cop21/rus/l09r.pdf (accessed on 3 January 2023).
7. Vladimir, L. K., & Vyacheslav, A. F., (2021). *The Fundamentals of Russia's Environmental Development Strategy*. Editorial research supervisors Dr. Moscow University Press.
8. Sasaev. (2022). *Strategic Analysis of Trends in the Development of the Russian Far East Gas Industry*.
9. Ibid.
10. Makarova, Y. V., (2018). Global gas market development: The role of LNG. *Intellect. Innovation. Investments, 3*, 31–36.
11. Chetverikov, V. M., (2020). Unique features and intensity of COVID-19 spread in large economies. *Voprosy Statistiki*, *27*(6), 86–104.
12. *Coronavirus Pandemic (COVID-19): The Data.* Our World in Data. https://ourworldindata.org/coronavirus-data#cases-and-deaths (accessed on 3 January 2023).
13. *There Is a Gloomy Forecast About the Development of the COVID-19 Pandemic*, (2021). MK.ru. https://www.mk.ru/science/2021/10/30/poyavilsya-mrachnyy-prognoz-po-povodu-razvitiya-pandemii-covid19.html (accessed on 3 January 2023).
14. Vladimir, L. K., (2021). *Strategizing of the Digital Kuzbass Region*. Editorial research supervisor. Kemerovo State University.
15. Shiplyuk, V. S., (2020). Digital contribution to economic growth. *Business Strategies*, *8*(12), 343–348.
16. *Digital Disruption: The Growth Multiplier*. Oxford Economics, http://www.oxfordeconomics.com/recent-releases/digital-disruption (accessed on 3 January 2023).
17. *Have the Townspeople Changed Internally? Digital Totals*, (2020). Global Affairs. https://globalaffairs.ru/articles/izmenilis-li-gorozhane-czifra-2020 (accessed on 3 January 2023).
18. Miroslavskaya, M. V., & Kozyrev, A. A., (2021). Digital Economy as a tool for sustainable development. *Administrative Consulting*, (3), 58–69.
19. Sasaev N. I., (2019). *Theoretical Foundations and Methodology of the Russian Gas Industry Development Strategy* (p. 176). SPb.: NWIM RANEPA, (In Russ.).
20. *Why Industrial Production is Moving from China to Southeast Asia,* (2015). Kommersant.ru. https://www.kommersant.ru/doc/2713978 (accessed on 3 January 2023).
21. *Outlook for Energy: A Perspective to 2040.* ExxonMobil. https://corporate.exxonmobil.com/Energy-and-innovation/outlook-for-energy (accessed on 3 January 2023).

22. *Insights on the Polymer Global Market to 2030: Industry Analysis and Growth Forecasts,* (2021). PR NewsWire. https://www.prnewswire.com/news-releases/insights-on-the-polymer-global-market-to-2030---industry-analysis-and-growth-forecasts-301336443.html (accessed on 3 January 2023).
23. *Polymer Development Trend,* (2021). CDU.ru. https://www.cdu.ru/tek_russia/issue/2021/3/882 (accessed on 3 January 2023).
24. Sasaev, N. I., & Kvint, V. L., (2019). Argument for development of processing and chemical production of gas as a strategic priority of Russian economy, St. Petersburg state Polytechnical University journal. *Economics, 12*(5), 102–116. doi: 10.18721/JE.12508.
25. *Shale Gas Production*. URL.: https://www.eia.gov/dnav/ng/ng_prod_shalegas_s1_a.htm (accessed on 3 January 2023).
26. *Gazprom Predicted a Drop in Shale Gas Production in the United States*, (2020). RBC.ru. https://www.rbc.ru/business/24/04/2020/5ea2a8779a79478d706ae32d (accessed on 3 January 2023).
27. *Import Substitution in the Fuel and Energy Complex*. https://minenergo.gov.ru/node/7693 (accessed on 3 January 2023).
28. *Ministry of Industry and Trade: The Share of Foreign Equipment in Oil and Gas Fell by 17%,* (2021). DProm Online. https://dprom.online/oilngas/dolya-importa-v-neftegaze-upala-na-17 (accessed on 3 January 2023).
29. *Revival of the Oil and Gas Equipment Market*, (2020). CDU.ru. https://www.cdu.ru/tek_russia/articles/1/804 (accessed on 3 January 2023).
30. *Digital Transformation of the Oil and Gas Industry*, (2021). CDU.ru. https://www.cdu.ru/tek_russia/articles/1/933 (accessed on 3 January 2023).
31. Sasaev, N. I., (2019). Diversification of natural gas export flows is the strategic priority for the development of the Russian gas industry. *The Economic Revival of Russia*, *3*(61), 185–196.
32. *Russian Ambassador to Beijing Spoke About Gas Supplies Through the Power of Siberia,* (2021). Ria.ru. https://ria.ru/20210210/postavki-1596879079.html (accessed on 3 January 2023).
33. Novikova, *The Russian Far East: Strategic Development of the Workforce*.
34. Serikov, S. G., & Ganina, T. N., (2021). Development of the Russian Far East and the Arctic: Demographic aspect. *Vestnik Universiteta*, (4), 79–86.
35. *Vladimir Putin Urged to Bring the Russian Far East to a Stable Positive Dynamics in Demography*, (2021). Tass.ru. https://tass.ru/obschestvo/12294167 (accessed on 3 January 2023).
36. *The Dynamics of Industrial Production in the Far East for January–May 2021 Was Analyzed by the Experts of the FANU "Vostokgosplan,"* (2021). http://assoc.khv.gov.ru (accessed on 3 January 2023).
37. *Prospects for Economic and Social Development of the Russian Far East Region*. https://www.presscentr.rbc.ru (accessed on 3 January 2023).
38. InfraOne Research, (2021). *"Investments in Infrastructure: The Far East.*" https://infraone-research.ru/vef2021/en/?utm_source=roscongress&utm_medium=banner&utm_campaign=vef2021&utm_content=landing+page (accessed on 18 January 2024).

39. *A Year of New Challenges. China Is Implementing 59 Projects in the Far Eastern Federal District*, (2021). RG.ru. https://rg.ru/2021/02/11/chislo-proektov-na-dalnem-vostoke-s-uchastiem-kitaia-vyroslo-do-59.html (accessed on 3 January 2023).
40. *Going to Our Equipment*, (2020). CDU.ru. https://www.cdu.ru/tek_russia/issue/2020/9/805 (accessed on 3 January 2023).
41. Yamal LNG's fourth train reaches full capacity, Kommersant reports (2021). Reuters. https://www.nasdaq.com/articles/yamal-lngs-fourth-train-reaches-full-capacity-kommersant-reports-2021-06-01 (accessed on 18 January 2024).
42. *TechnoChayanda: Efficient Technology at a Unique Field*, (2021). Neftegaz. https://neftegaz.ru/science/booty/693914-tekhnochayanda-effektivnaya-tekhnologiya-na-unikalnom-mestorozhdenii-/ (accessed on 3 January 2023).
43. *For Sakhalin-3. Gazprom Signed an Agreement with the Almaz-Antey Concern for the Localization of Serial Production of Underwater Oil and Gas Production Complexes*, (2019). Neftegaz. https://neftegaz.ru/news/Oborudovanie/194625-dlya-sakhalin-3-gazprom-podpisal-dogovor-s-kontsernom-almaz-antey-na-lokalizatsiyu-seriynogo-proizvo (accessed on 3 January 2023).
44. Fadeev, A. M., (2020). Implementation of energy projects on the Arctic shelf as a driver of socio-economic development of territories. *Economics, Resources, Finance, 3*, 56–63.

CHAPTER 5

Strategic Opportunities for the Development of the Russian Far East Gas Industry

5.1 ENSURING GASIFICATION OF THE RUSSIAN FAR EAST REGIONS

5.1.1 STRATEGIC OPPORTUNITIES JUSTIFYING ENSURING GASIFICATION OF THE RUSSIAN FAR EAST SUBJECTS AS A STRATEGIC DIRECTION

5.1.1.1 HIGH POTENTIAL FOR GASIFICATION OF THE FAR EASTERN FEDERAL DISTRICT SUBJECTS

The results of strategic diagnostics of the Far Eastern Federal District's gas industry show that the Republic of Sakha (Yakutia), the Sakhalin Region, the Khabarovsk Krai, and the Kamchatka Krai remain the leaders in gasification in the region [1]. Nevertheless, in five regions out of 11 (Magadan, Amur, and Jewish Autonomous Regions, Republic of Buryatia, and Zabaykalsky Krai), the level of gasification is still at zero, as a result of which the overall level of gasification in the Russian Far East does not exceed 20% (while the all-Russian level of gasification for 2021 is 71.4%) [2].

Meanwhile, a significant share of electricity generation in the Russian Far East is generated by thermal power plants, so for 2020, it was 61.3% for the unified energy system of the East, and 56.6% for isolated energy systems (Figure 5.1).

Strategizing the Russian Gas Industry: The Far Eastern Vector. Nikita I. Sasaev (Ed)

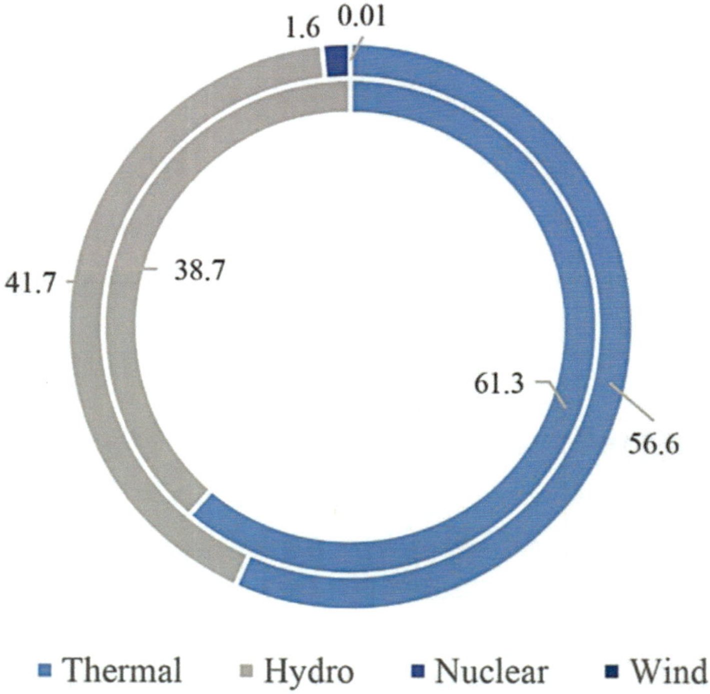

FIGURE 5.1 Structure of electricity generation in the Russian Far East in 2020.

Note: The inner circle represents the United Energy System of the Russian East, and the outer circle represents isolated systems of the Russian Far East.

Source: Compiled by the author based on "How the Russian Energy Balance Works" [3].

At the same time, in the fuel category of the unified energy system of the East, about 60–70% is coal, while in separate isolated systems, for example in the Magadan energy system, it exceeds 80% [4]. In turn, the degree of fixed asset depreciation in the unified energy system of the East reaches 45%, for isolated systems it is up to 49%.

5.1.1.2 ENVIRONMENTAL REQUEST FOR GASIFICATION

In accordance with the approved "Strategy for the Socio-economic Development of the Russian Federation with Low Greenhouse Gas Emissions Until 2050," net greenhouse gas emissions by 2050 should be reduced by 60% compared to 2019, and by 2060 it is expected to achieve carbon neutrality [5].

In addition, strategic initiatives are being developed and proposed at the national level, the implementation of which will allow not only to achieve the established targets but also to consolidate Russia's status as a leader-translator in the implementation of measures to reduce emissions of pollutants into the atmosphere [6].

At first glance, in the Far Eastern Federal District, the volume of emissions of pollutants from stationary sources (including thermal power plants), in relation to the all-Russian indicators, remains quite small (6.6% for 2020) (Table 5.1).

TABLE 5.1 Air Pollutant Emissions from Stationary Sources (1,000 Tons)

	2015	2016	2017	2018	2019	2020
Russian Federation	17,296	17,349	17,477	17,068	17,295	16,952
Far Eastern Federal District	1,115	1,085	1,147	1,026	1,099	1120.2
The Republic of Buryatia	109	94	113	93	96	94
The Republic of Sakha (Yakutia)	287	257	244	256	288	286.3
Zabaykalsky Krai	119	122	134	104	111	137.2
Kamchatka Krai	25	29	38	41	38	38.9
Primorsky Krai	193	186	186	181	178	169.7
Khabarovsk Krai	116	114	118	84	112	121.3
Amur Region	127	135	133	113	124	135.6
Magadan Region	27	31	33	29	60	39.8
Sakhalin Region	72	77	105	85	57	63.6
Jewish Autonomous Region	19	19	23	19	16	16.5
Chukotka Autonomous Region	21	21	20	23	18	17.3

Source: Compiled by the author based on the Federal State Statistics Service.

Taking into account a low population with a large territorial area (5.56% of the country's population is located within 40.6% of the entire territory of Russia), as a result of which population density remains the lowest (1.17 people on km^2) [7], it is necessary to compare average per capita indicators, for which the FEFD still exceeds the Russian average (Table 5.2) [8].

TABLE 5.2 Air Pollutant Emissions from Stationary Sources per Person (Tons)

Region	2015	2020	Change from 2015 to 2020 (%)
Russian Federation	0.118	0.116	98%
Far Eastern Federal District	0.151	0.138	91%
The Republic of Buryatia	0.098	0.095	97%
The Republic of Sakha (Yakutia)	0.301	0.293	98%
Zabaykalsky Krai	0.102	0.130	127%
Kamchatka Krai	0.120	0.125	104%
Primorsky Krai	0.092	0.090	98%
Khabarovsk Krai	0.084	0.093	111%
Amur Region	0.154	0.173	112%
Magadan Region	0.408	0.285	70%
Sakhalin Region	0.117	0.131	112%
Jewish Autonomous Region	0.096	0.105	110%
Chukotka Autonomous Region	0.358	0.347	97%

Source: Compiled by the author based on the Federal State Statistics Service.

Meanwhile, air pollution is one of the most pressing problems at the regional and municipal levels [9]. A number of cities in the Russian Far East are included in the lists of cities with the most polluted air [10]. In turn, the population of the Far Eastern Federal District is fully interested in improving the environmental situation, including through the gasification of the regions [11]. On the contrary, persistent environmental problems only reinforce the dynamics of the population outflow from the Far Eastern Federal District.

All this opens up an ecological window of opportunity to ensure the gasification of Far Eastern Federal District regions.

5.1.2 STRATEGIC THREATS THAT POTENTIALLY IMPEDE THE IMPLEMENTATION OF THE STRATEGIC DIRECTION "ENSURING GASIFICATION OF RUSSIAN FAR EAST REGIONS"

No significant strategic threats to the implementation of the strategic direction for ensuring the gasification of Russian Far East regions in the medium and long term have been identified, however, a number of potential ones can be noted in the longer term [8]:

- Decrease in the level of gas production in the Far Eastern Federal District (as a result of the depletion of gas fields beyond the 50-year perspective).

- Cardinal deterioration of socio-economic conditions in the region (as a consequence of a critical outflow of the population and/or a critical decline in production).
- Obsolescence of the technological base (non-compliance of the level of technology with the requirements for the development of fields, including hard-to-recover reserves).
- Replacement with alternative energy (emergence of new efficient alternative energy sources; for example, thermonuclear fusion energy).

5.2 DEVELOPMENT OF GAS PROCESSING AND GAS CHEMISTRY IN THE RUSSIAN FAR EAST

5.2.1 STRATEGIC OPPORTUNITIES JUSTIFYING THE DEVELOPMENT OF GAS PROCESSING AND GAS CHEMISTRY IN THE RUSSIAN FAR EAST AS A STRATEGIC DIRECTION

5.2.1.1 GROWING GLOBAL DEMAND FOR HELIUM

Helium production should become an important strategic direction in the development of gas processing in the Russian Far East. This strategic opportunity is underpinned by a number of strategic factors, the first of which is related to the rapid growth in global demand for helium coupled with strong demand from the aerospace and electronics industries. According to some estimates, it is predicted that by 2024 demand for helium will increase by more than 21% [12]; according to other more optimistic estimates the helium market will grow faster over this period, so the average annual growth rate will be 11% [13]. Secondly, Russia occupies a low share of world helium production (4–4.5 million cubic meters), having only one Orenburg helium plant, significantly inferior to the USA (74 million cubic meters), Qatar (45 million cubic meters), and Algeria (14 million cubic meters). However, it is noted that the United States has already reduced helium exports from 2012 to 2020 by more than 59 million cubic meters and may continue to decline after 2023 [14, 15], which opens up additional opportunities for Russia to increase production capacity and enter the global helium market. Based on the fact that the Far Eastern Federal District has the largest helium reserves in Russia [16], it can become a driver in this strategic direction as well. It should be noted that active work is already underway in Russia in this direction, as the Amur gas processing plant project is being implemented with a design capacity for helium production of up to 60 million cubic meters per year [17], however, given the rapidly growing market and resource opportunities, it is advisable to continue increasing helium production and consolidation of leadership positions in the rapidly developing Asia-Pacific region.

5.2.1.2 IMPORT SUBSTITUTION OF CHEMICAL PRODUCTS

Products of the chemical industry are an essential component for the functioning of many industries, which is one of the strategic factors that ensure the economic security of the state. Thus, in accordance with the approved "Strategy for the Development of the Chemical and Petrochemical Complex for the Period up to 2030," one of the goals is to strengthen national security by providing the military-industrial complex and strategic industries with high-quality domestic chemical products [18].

Increasing the production capacity of the domestic chemical industry from 2014 to 2020 generally reduced the share of imports to 16% [19], however, the dependence on imports for the main groups of polymers is still high (Table 5.3).

TABLE 5.3 Imports by Russia of the Main Groups of Polymers from 2016 to 2020 (1,000 Tons)

2016	2017	2018	2019	2020
Polymers of Ethylene (in Primary Forms)				
554.5	650.1	655.1	839.9	674.1
Polymers of Propylene or Other Olefins (in Primary Forms)				
197.4	210.5	231.7	228.8	262.9
Polymers of Styrene (in Primary Forms)				
126.6	124.3	120.7	138.1	126.3
Polymers of Vinyl Acetate or Other Vinyl Esters (in Primary Forms; Other Vinyl Polymers; in Primary Forms)				
48.9	47.9	50.4	53.5	52.1
Polymers of Vinyl Chloride or Other Halogenated Olefins (in Primary Forms)				
272.9	198.5	147.4	218.5	201.3
Acrylic Polymers (in Primary Forms)				
183.4	201.1	206.2	216.3	210.4
Polyacetals, Other Polyethers and Epoxide Resins (in Primary Forms; Polycarbonates, Alkyd Resins, Polyallyl Esters, and Other Polyesters; in Primary Forms)				
414.8	429.6	491.5	549.8	543.2

Source: Compiled by the author based on The International Trade Center database.

Despite the peculiarities of the global chemical products market, the impact of the pandemic, as well as the high volatility of energy prices in 2021, the window of opportunity for import substitution of chemical industry products at the expense of oil and gas chemistry has remained [20].

In addition, given the presence of such a significant competitive advantage for the Far Eastern gas industry as the presence of natural gas reserves containing significant amounts of valuable components in its composition, primarily helium and ethane [1, 21], it can become a driver for the development of domestic gas chemistry in a wide range of promising directions [22, 23]. This is true, for example, in the production of polyethylene and polypropylene, the consumption in Russia will increase by 1 million tons by 2030 and amount to 4.4 million tons per year [24].

It should be noted that a large-scale project is already being implemented in the Russian Far East for the construction and launch of the largest enterprise for the production of polyethylene and polypropylene (Amur Gas Chemical Complex). Its production capacity will be 2.3 million tons of polyethylene and 0.4 million tons of polypropylene per year [25]. Without a doubt, this enterprise will have a system-forming character not only for the economy of the Far Eastern Federal District but also for the economy of eastern Russia [26]. Nevertheless, taking into account resource opportunities, growth prospects for the Russian economy, as well as a number of strategic factors that ensure the long-term development of domestic gas chemistry (including the replacement of traditional materials with composite ones) [27], it is necessary to continue increasing production capacities in these directions.

5.2.1.3 GROWING GLOBAL DEMAND FOR PETROCHEMICAL PRODUCTS

In addition to providing the Russian market with high-quality domestic gas chemical products, there is a strategic opportunity to increase its exports. First of all, this is due to increasing growth in the corresponding chemical products. For example, from 2011 to 2020, the total demand for imported ethylene polymers in primary forms increased by more than 1.65 times and amounted to about 64 million tons per year, and for imported propylene polymers by 1.16 times and exceeded 29.4 million tons per year. At the same time, the largest contribution was made by China, where the demand for imported ethylene polymers in primary forms over the same period increased by 2.6 times to 21.27 million tons per year, and for imported propylene polymers by 1.38 times to 6.84 million tons per year (Table 5.4).

TABLE 5.4 Top Five Importing Countries of the Main Polymer Groups for 2020 (Million Tons)

Polymers of Ethylene (in Primary Forms)					
	China	**USA**	**Belgium**	**Germany**	**Singapore**
2011	8.194	2.800	2.081	2.558	1.669
2020	21.277	3.456	2.726	2.661	2.473
Polymers of Propylene or Other Olefins (in Primary Forms)					
	China	Turkey	Italy	Germany	Vietnam
2011	4.936	1.487	1.583	1.631	0.639
2020	6.840	2.496	1.776	1.767	1.181
Polymers of Vinyl Chloride or Other Halogenated Olefins (in Primary Forms)					
	India	China	Turkey	Italy	Germany
2011	0.833	1.390	0.855	0.787	0.706
2020	1.782	1.258	0.796	0.706	0.687
Polyacetals, Other Polyethers, and Epoxide Resins (in Primary Forms; Polycarbonates, Alkyd Resins, Polyallyl Esters, and Other Polyesters; in Primary Forms)					
	China	USA	India	Germany	France
2011	0.142	0.085	0.060	0.141	0.078
2020	0.205	0.131	0.129	0.128	0.102

Source: Compiled by the author based on The International Trade Center database.

According to P&S Intelligence experts, the annual growth of global demand for polymers will be 5.1% until 2030, as a result of which the volume of the polymer market in value terms will exceed $838 billion (1.57 times more than in 2019). It is noted that due to the accelerated development of construction, the automotive industry, the electronics industry (the main consumers of polymers), etc., it is the Asia-Pacific region that will grow at the fastest pace [28], which is another justification for the need to increase the corresponding gas chemical capacities in the Russian Far East to implement this strategic opportunity.

At the same time, it is worth noting that in 2020 Russia accounted for only 1.69% of the global export of ethylene polymers in primary forms, yielding even to France (2.16%), which does not have such an extensive raw material base. Therefore, the introduction of new facilities, in addition to the Amur Gas Chemical Complex, should be considered a strategically important opportunity not only to reach the planned volumes of polymer exports [19] but also to take a leading position in the world.

5.2.2 STRATEGIC THREATS THAT POTENTIALLY IMPEDE THE IMPLEMENTATION OF THE STRATEGIC DIRECTION "DEVELOPMENT OF GAS PROCESSING AND GAS CHEMICAL PRODUCTION IN THE RUSSIAN FAR EAST"

5.2.2.1 COMPETITION FROM OTHER PRODUCING COUNTRIES

The most significant strategic threat to the development of gas processing and gas chemistry in the Russian Far East is competition from other market participants. For example, there is a high level of competition in the market of ethylene polymers in primary forms, where over the past 10 years the leading positions in the export of this group of products have been occupied by the United States, which increased exports by 2.45 times over this period; Saudi Arabia, which increased export capacities by 1.5 times; Singapore (1.5 times export growth); Belgium (1.14 times); and South Korea (1.61 times).

Exports of propylene polymers and other olefins in primary forms are steadily leading Saudi Arabia, South Korea, Belgium, Singapore, and Germany. At the same time, only Saudi Arabia (by 1.61 times) and South Korea (by 1.41 times) significantly increased their exports. It is also important to note that the United Arab Emirates and Malaysia were among the new potential competitors, increasing their share in the export of polypropylene from an insignificant level to 5.01% and 3.52%, respectively (Table 5.5).

TABLE 5.5 Share of Leading Exporting Countries of Some Forms of Polymers for 2011 and 2020 (%)

Polymers of Ethylene (in Primary Forms)			Polymers of Propylene or Other Olefins (in Primary Forms)		
Country	**2011**	**2020**	**Country**	**2011**	**2020**
USA	9.78%	17.77%	Saudi Arabia	12.23%	15.56%
Saudi Arabia	14.18%	15.79%	South Korea	9.39%	10.46%
Singapore	6.47%	7.68%	Belgium	9.44%	8.50%
Belgium	7.57%	6.43%	Singapore	6.53%	6.57%
South Korea	4.96%	5.92%	Germany	7.43%	6.43%
Canada	6.21%	5.80%	USA	7.79%	6.34%
Thailand	4.60%	4.55%	UAE	0.00%	5.01%
Iran	3.49%	4.23%	Netherlands	4.09%	3.58%
Germany	4.70%	3.92%	Malaysia	0.90%	3.52%
Netherlands	4.20%	3.64%	Thailand	2.96%	3.47%
Malaysia	1.43%	3.40%	France	4.21%	3.13%
France	2.91%	2.16%	Chinese Taipei	2.64%	3.07%
India	0.63%	1.70%	India	3.16%	2.75%
Russian Federation	0.50%	1.69%	Russian Federation	0.12%	2.26%
Total Other Countries	28.37%	15.32%	Total Other Countries	29.11%	19.34%

Source: Compiled by the author based on The International Trade Center database.

According to the mid-term forecast "Global Polyethylene Industry Outlook to 2024—Capacity and Capital Expenditure Forecasts with Details of All Active and Planned Plants," which takes into account the introduction of about 154 planned and announced plants for the production of polyethylene, the global production capacity for this product will increase by 52% to 173.55 million tons per year by 2024 [29]. Thus, potential competitors' production capacities will increase by more than 45 million tons of polyethylene per year, while about 50–60% of the commissioned capacities will be in Asia-Pacific countries, including China, India, Indonesia, and South Korea.

A similar situation is predicted for the global production of polypropylene. Taking into account the commissioning of all the 146 planned and announced plants by 2025, global production capacity for polypropylene will increase by 60% to 136.7 million tons per year [30]. At the same time, Asia will provide about 80% of the increase in production, and just like

China during this period is planned to build 46 plants, which will increase production by 19 million tons of propylene per year.

Meanwhile, in the long term and from the point of view of the existing raw material base, only the United States, Saudi Arabia, and Iran will be able to compete with Russian exports in these positions.

Competition will also intensify in the helium market, as by 2030 the world supply will increase by 1.52 times compared to 2020 and will amount to approximately 260 million cubic meters per year, while the list of potential competitor countries will not change [15]. The main competition is expected from Qatar, which plans to more than double its production capacity.

However, this strategic threat can only slow down the implementation of strategic opportunities for the development of gas processing and gas chemical production in the Russian Far East, which is due to the presence of significant competitive advantages (the largest raw material base and strategic proximity to the main sales markets).

5.3 NETWORK GAS EXPORTS

5.3.1 STRATEGIC OPPORTUNITIES THAT JUSTIFY THE EXPORT OF NETWORK GAS AS A STRATEGIC DIRECTION OF THE RUSSIAN FAR EAST GAS INDUSTRY

The monitoring process revealed two significant strategic opportunities that make this strategic direction promising for the Russian Far East gas industry in the long term [31].

5.3.1.1 THE ASIA-PACIFIC REGION AS AN ENERGY WINDOW OF OPPORTUNITY

The high economic growth rates of a number of countries in the Asia-Pacific region, as well as the strategic trend associated with the shift of industrial centers in favor of the Asia-Pacific region, determined the long-term leadership of the region in terms of primary energy consumption (in 2020, the Asia-Pacific region accounted for about 45.5% of global energy consumption) [32]. China, India, Japan, and South Korea remain the main energy-consuming countries in the Asia-Pacific region (Table 5.6).

TABLE 5.6 Dynamics of the Energy Balance Structure of Asia-Pacific Countries from 2000 to 2020 (Exajoules)

Country	Year	Primary Energy Consumption	Natural Gas Consumption	Coal Consumption	Oil Consumption	Nuclear Energy Consumption	Hydropower Consumption	Renewable Energy Consumption	Share of Energy Received from "Clean" Sources
China	2000	42.5	0.9	29.6	9.6	0.2	2.2	0.0	8%
	2010	104.3	3.9	73.2	19.0	0.7	6.7	0.7	12%
	2020	145.5	11.9	82.3	28.5	3.3	11.7	7.7	24%
India	2000	13.4	0.9	6.9	4.6	0.2	0.8	0.0	14%
	2010	22.5	2.1	12.2	6.6	0.2	1.0	0.3	16%
	2020	32.0	2.1	17.5	9.0	0.4	1.5	1.3	17%
Japan	2000	22.3	2.7	4.0	11.4	3.2	0.8	0.2	31%
	2010	21.1	3.6	4.9	8.8	2.7	0.8	0.3	35%
	2020	17.0	3.8	4.6	6.5	0.4	0.7	1.1	35%
South Korea	2000	7.9	0.7	1.8	4.3	1.1	0.0	0.0	23%
	2010	10.8	1.6	3.2	4.5	1.4	0.0	0.0	29%
	2020	11.8	2.0	3.0	4.9	1.4	0.0	0.3	32%
Other Asia-Pacific countries	2000	26.4	5.5	5.8	13.1	0.4	1.3	0.2	28%
	2010	37.9	9.5	8.9	17.0	0.4	1.7	0.4	32%
	2020	47.5	11.2	13.6	18.2	0.4	2.5	1.3	32%
Total Asia-Pacific	2000	112.5	10.7	48.0	43.0	5.0	5.2	0.5	19%
	2010	196.6	20.7	102.3	55.8	5.5	10.3	1.8	19%
	2020	253.7	31.0	121.0	67.1	5.8	16.4	11.7	26%

Note: "Clean" energy sources are – natural gas, nuclear, hydro, and alternative energy.
Source: Compiled by the author based on BP's "Energy Outlook: 2020 Edition."

BP's long-term forecasts assume that, under a realistic scenario, global energy consumption will increase by more than 25% by 2050, with Asian countries primarily making a positive contribution to growth—primarily India (increasing energy consumption by 2.5 times) and China (increasing by 1.14 times) [33]. Additionally, according to the International Energy Agency, under a scenario that takes into account the implementation of the declared energy security policy by Asian countries, world energy consumption will increase by 13% by 2030 and by 26% by 2050; energy consumption in the Asia-Pacific region will increase by 18% by 2030 and 29% by 2050 [34]. India will make a significant contribution to the growth of regional consumption, which by 2050 will increase energy consumption by 1.89 times compared to 2020. Experts also assume that China, having increased energy consumption by 11% by 2030, will reach a peak value, after which it will slightly reduce energy consumption by 2050.

Meanwhile, the natural gas market is noted as promising in the region and the demand for natural gas in the Asia-Pacific region will increase by 1.71 times by 2050, in India by 3.28 times, and in China by 1.6 times (Figure 5.2).

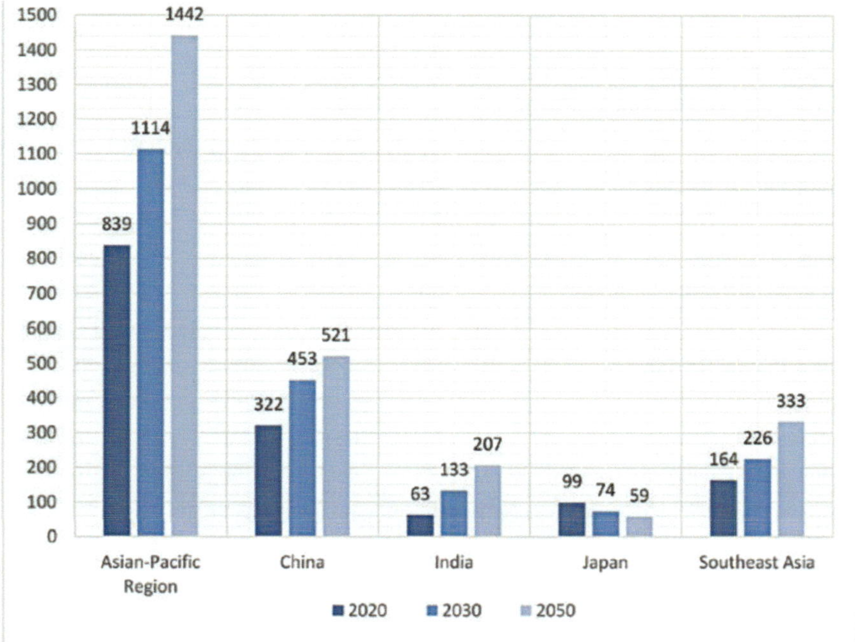

FIGURE 5.2 Projected demand for natural gas in the Asia-Pacific region by 2030 and 2050 (bcm).

Source: Compiled by the author based on World Energy Outlook (2021); IEA.

Along with this, according to the IEA, the growth of the domestic supply of natural gas in the Asia-Pacific region will be significantly inferior to consumption. Regional gas production will amount to 702 billion cubic meters by 2030 and 782 billion cubic meters by 2050; all this will determine a significant share of unsecured demand for natural gas in the domestic energy market of the Asia-Pacific region (36.9% and 45.7%, respectively) [35].

BP's optimistic forecast notes that demand for natural gas in the region will increase by 1.82 times by 2050, while natural gas consumption in China will increase by 2.04 times, and in India by more than 4.25 times in relation to 2020 (Table 5.7).

TABLE 5.7 Forecast Estimates of Domestic Demand and Supply of Natural Gas in the Asia-Pacific Region until 2050

	2025	2030	2035	2040	2045	2050
	Domestic Demand for Natural Gas (Billion Cubic Meters)					
Asian-Pacific Region	1,108	1,303	1,410	1,486	1,539	1,575
China	490	601	651	677	685	675
India	88	123	156	187	219	254
Other Asia-Pacific countries	310	352	383	408	429	441
	Domestic Supply of Natural Gas (Billion Cubic Meters)					
Asian-Pacific Region	715	705	737	742	773	745
China	241	273	305	325	355	345
India	47	49	53	62	82	96
Other Asia-Pacific countries	269	230	212	192	176	147
	Share of Unsecured Demand for Natural Gas					
Asian-Pacific Region	35%	46%	48%	50%	50%	53%
China	51%	55%	53%	52%	48%	49%
India	47%	60%	66%	67%	63%	62%
Other Asia-Pacific countries	13%	35%	45%	53%	59%	67%

Source: Compiled by the author based on BP's "Energy Outlook: 2020 Edition."

Thus, the Asia-Pacific region can be viewed as an energy window of opportunity, where the natural gas market, with a high share of unsecured demand by domestic supply, is certainly a promising strategic direction for expanding gas exports from the Russian Far East.

5.3.1.2 *ECOLOGICAL WINDOW OF OPPORTUNITY IN THE ASIA-PACIFIC REGION*

In accordance with the adopted Paris Agreement, and in order to reverse the global trend of "climate change," which includes negative environmental changes including those related to pollutant emissions, a number of programs and policies are being developed and adopted at the regional level. For the most part, all policy documents to one degree or another relate to the transition to a low-carbon economy as a rule, including a move away from the use of "dirty" energy sources in favor of environmentally friendly and renewable ones. This also concerns the Asia-Pacific region, which over the past 20 years has been the leader in carbon dioxide emissions (51% of global carbon dioxide emissions in 2020) [31].

Particularly noteworthy is China's policy (China is the largest emitter of carbon dioxide—30.7% in 2020), which is associated with energy development and the simultaneous reduction of pollutant emissions. China's "14th Five-Year Socio-Economic Development Plan," with long-term goals up to 2035, sets a target for peaking the country's CO_2 emissions by 2030 and a goal of achieving carbon neutrality by 2060 [36]. It is planned to achieve these targets by the specified deadline by building a low-carbon, safe, and efficient energy system, as well as by accelerating the development of non-fossil energy sources with an increase in their share in the energy balance up to 20%. Despite this, in order to ensure China's energy security, it is necessary to stimulate the exploration of oil and gas fields and increase gas and oil production, as well as a diversified expansion of sources of oil and gas imports while maintaining safe strategic channels and key energy hubs.

The Indian government is also interested in reducing greenhouse gas emissions. Thus, in accordance with the Paris Agreement, it is planned to transfer 40% of the electricity generation capacity to non-fossil fuel sources by 2030, having fulfilled ahead of schedule one of the obligations assumed under the agreement [37]. However, given that around 60% of India's thermal power plants are coal-fired, natural gas could be one viable option to achieve the intended target of reducing pollutant emissions [38].

Ambitious goals for the transition to a low-carbon economy by the 1950s and 1960s in China, India, and a number of other Asia-Pacific countries open an environmental window of opportunity to expand the use of natural gas in the region and provide a long-term strategic opportunity for the gas industry in the Russian Far East.

5.3.2 STRATEGIC THREATS HINDERING THE IMPLEMENTATION OF THE STRATEGIC DIRECTION (GAS EXPORTATION FROM THE RUSSIAN FAR EAST)

The formulation of a strategic direction is impossible without identifying and evaluating strategic threats that can limit the implementation of the strategic opportunities that form it.

5.3.2.1 COMPETITION IN THE NATURAL GAS MARKET IN THE ASIA-PACIFIC REGION

The most realistic threat to the implementation of the identified strategic opportunities in this area is the growing competition in the network natural gas market in the Asia-Pacific region. If in 2010 the main gas suppliers were Indonesia (35%), Myanmar (31%), and Turkmenistan (13%), then by 2020, in addition to the fact that the leader-supplier of gas to the market has changed, it has become Turkmenistan (42%), with the traditional main suppliers of Indonesia (11%) and Myanmar (17%) being joined by Kazakhstan (10%), the Russian Federation (6%), and Uzbekistan (5%) (Figure 5.3).

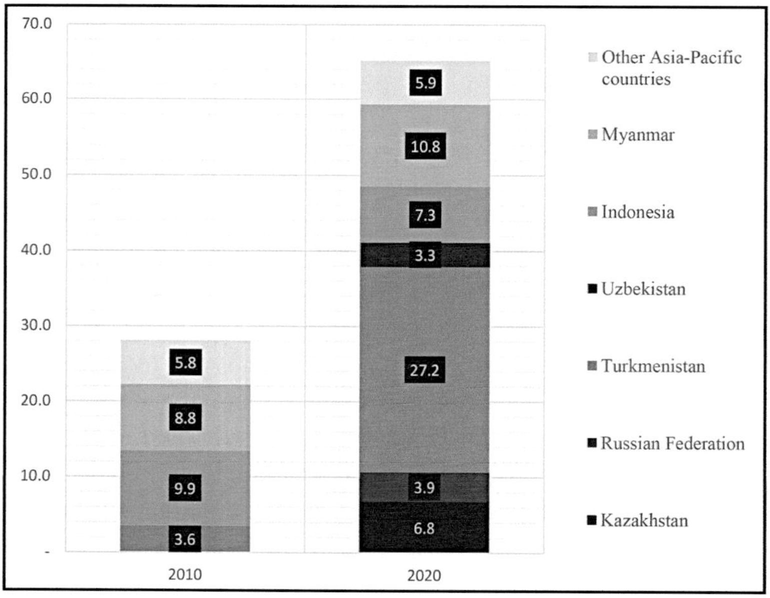

FIGURE 5.3 Importers of pipeline natural gas in the Asia-Pacific region for 2010 and 2020 (bcm).

Source: Compiled by the author based on BP's "Energy Outlook: 2020 Edition."

Based on an assessment of resource capabilities, namely the natural gas reserves of the listed supplier countries, the only long-term and significant competitor for Russia in this area is Turkmenistan, which has about 13.6 trillion cubic meters of proven gas reserves [32].

5.3.2.2 *COMPETITION FROM ALTERNATIVE ENERGY SOURCES*

The course taken by countries to achieve low levels of pollutant emissions strengthens the trend toward a transformation in the energy market and stimulates an increase in the share of "clean" energy sources in national energy balances by increasing the consumption of environmentally friendly and alternative energy resources, including hydro and nuclear energy, and to a greater extent renewable energy sources (RES).

However, an analysis of the forecasts for a net zero scenario (full implementation of measures and policies that provide for a 95% reduction in emissions compared to 2018) and business-as-usual scenario (continuation of national development trajectories, including those that contribute to reducing greenhouse gas emissions by 10% compared to 2018), shows that by 2050, in both the first scenario (the share of energy received from RES is 60%) and the second (the share of energy received from RES is 21%), the share of energy that will be obtained on the basis of natural gas will be steadily 13–16%, with nuclear and hydropower at 6–9% (Table 5.8) [33].

The development of alternative energy sources is not a direct strategic threat that completely excludes natural gas from the energy balances in the region, and to a greater extent, it can only slow down the growth of natural gas consumption in the region [31].

5.3.2.3 *SUBSTITUTION OF IMPORTED GAS IN THE ASIA-PACIFIC REGION AT THE EXPENSE OF DOMESTIC SOURCES*

From the point of view of the potential for developing gas sources, one can note the resource potential that the Asia-Pacific region has, namely 16.6 trillion cubic meters of proven gas reserves for 2020 (8.8% of the world), while 50% of them are concentrated in China (the increase in gas production is determined by the above 14th national five-year plan) [32]. In India, in response to the high share of imported LNG in the country's energy

TABLE 5.8 Forecast Estimates of Energy Production from "Clean" Energy Sources in the Energy Balances of the Asia-Pacific Region (Exajoules)

		Baseline	Net Zero Scenario		Business-as-Usual Scenario	
Source	**Country/Region**	**2018**	**2030**	**2050**	**2030**	**2050**
Primary energy consumption	Asian-Pacific region	249	297	316	306	349
	China	136	155	139	159	155
	India	34	53	77	54	86
	Other Asia-Pacific countries	41	54	68	56	76
Natural gas	Asian-Pacific region	30	43	42	47	57
	China	10	19	19	22	24
	India	2	6	9	4	9
	Other Asia-Pacific countries	10	12	10	13	16
Nuclear power	Asian-Pacific region	5	12	29	10	20
	China	3	6	17	6	14
	India	0	1	5	1	3
	Other Asia-Pacific countries	0	1	2	0	1
Hydro energy	Asian-Pacific region	15	21	28	20	23
	China	11	13	17	13	14
	India	1	2	3	2	2
	Other Asia-Pacific countries	2	4	7	4	5
Solar energy	Asian-Pacific region	3	25	83	12	29
	China	2	13	36	8	13
	India	0	5	26	2	9
	Other Asia-Pacific countries	0	2	12	0	3
Wind energy	Asian-Pacific region	4	26	79	15	33
	China	3	15	31	11	19
	India	1	6	20	2	8
	Other Asia-Pacific countries	0	2	21	0	4
Biomass energy	Asian-Pacific region	2	14	27	5	9
	China	1	7	10	3	4
	India	0	3	8	1	2
	Other Asia-Pacific countries	1	3	7	1	2

Source: Compiled by the author based on BP's "Energy Outlook: 2020 Edition."

balance, it is planned to increase gas production in the Bay of Bengal during the medium term [39].

In addition to traditional sources, non-traditional gas sources are in active development, primarily shale gas, the largest regional reserves of which are also in China [22]. If the long-term plan is fulfilled, it will be able to receive an additional 80–100 billion cubic meters of gas from shale per year by 2030, while simultaneously replacing its imports. However, the achievement of the target may be questionable, given the negative impact of hydraulic fracturing technology in the production of gas from shale, while the opposite national goal is set to improve the environment in China.

Of particular interest are gas hydrates or clathrates, the reserves of which are in China (the northern region of the South China Sea), India (the Bay of Bengal), and Japan (the Nankai trough) [40]. China and Japan are already conducting research in the field of hydrated methane production [41], but the existing production technologies make it unprofitable.

The development of traditional and non-traditional gas sources in the Asia-Pacific region in order to replace the import of this energy resource is one of the significant strategic threats to the development of a strategic direction for expanding natural gas exports from the Russian Far East to the Asia-Pacific region. Nevertheless, it is able to exert the greatest degree of influence only in the long and ultra-long term, which is due to the dependence on technological and technical development in the production of such energy resources in the Asia-Pacific region.

5.4 LIQUEFIED NATURAL GAS PRODUCTION

5.4.1 MAIN RESULTS OF THE ANALYSIS OF STRATEGIC OPPORTUNITIES THAT JUSTIFY THE DEVELOPMENT OF LARGE-SCALE LNG PRODUCTION IN THE RUSSIAN FAR EAST

5.4.1.1 GROWING DEMAND FOR LNG

The disproportionate distribution of natural gas reserves by regions of the world and the growing trend of transformation in the energy market associated with withdrawal from "dirty" energy sources, including the transition to natural gas, determine the formation of a global natural gas market by increasing the share of interregional trade in liquefied natural gas [42].

Over the past two decades alone, the volume of LNG trade has increased by more than 3.4 times and amounted to 487.9 billion cubic meters in 2020, while the main importing regions and consumers of liquefied natural gas are the Asia-Pacific Region (71% of all world LNG imports) and Europe (24%) (Figure 5.4).

In accordance with the International Energy Agency's medium-term forecast, the volume of imports and consumption of LNG will continue to grow rapidly and by 2025 will increase by 20% [43]. According to long-term estimates, demand for liquefied natural gas is expected to grow in the range of 25–50% by 2030 [44]. In turn, Shell experts believe that by 2040 the demand for LNG will double and amount to about 952 billion cubic meters per year [45].

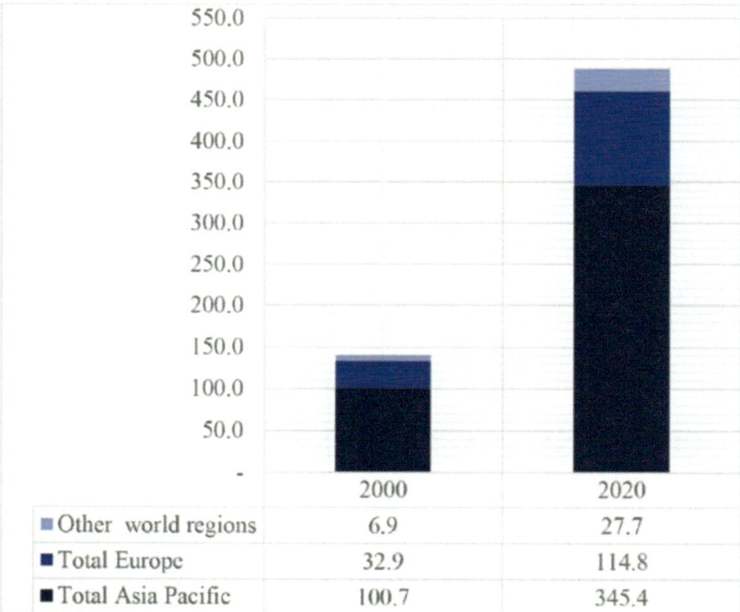

FIGURE 5.4 Regional structure of imports and consumption of LNG (bcm).

Source: Compiled by the author based on the BP database.

All of the above sources indicate that the Asia-Pacific region will remain the leader in imports and consumption of LNG. Analyzing the dynamics and structure of LNG imports in the Asia-Pacific region, it can be noted that almost all countries in the region, with the exception of

Japan, increased the consumption of liquefied natural gas throughout the study period. The leaders in this indicator for 2020 were Japan, China, South Korea, and India (Figure 5.5).

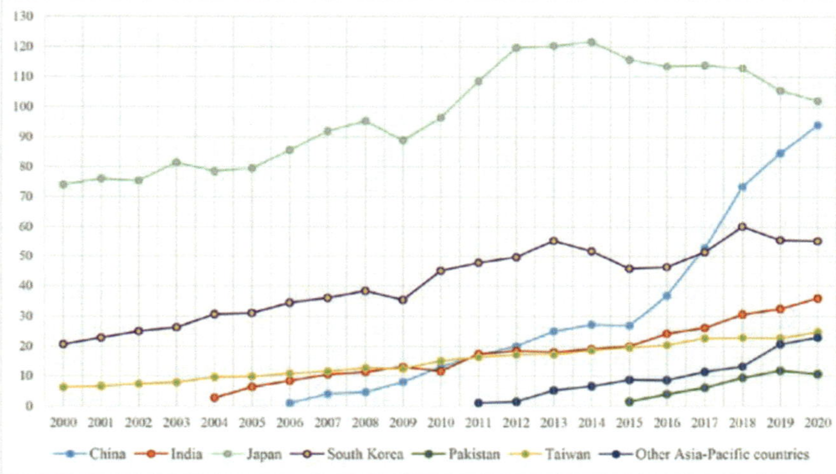

FIGURE 5.5 Dynamics of LNG imports by Asia-Pacific countries (bcm).

Source: Compiled by the author based on the BP database.

China, India, Taiwan, Thailand, and Bangladesh are considered among the main drivers of LNG demand growth [46].

At the same time, the long-term leaders in the consumption of liquefied natural gas in the region will be China, which will increase consumption to 176.8 billion cubic meters per year by 2040 [45], and India, which plans to increase LNG imports by 2040 to over 130 billion cubic meters per year [46].

Thus, a strategic opportunity opens up for the Russian Far East to expand LNG exports to the Asia-Pacific region in the long term [42].

5.4.1.2 GOVERNMENT INCENTIVES AND SUPPORT

The prospects and significance of developing the liquefaction of natural gas in Russia and its exports are supported by long-term government incentives and support. First of all, it is worth noting the "Long-term Program for the Development of Liquefied Natural Gas Production in the Russian Federation" approved in 2021 [47].

Active support measures include tax breaks and incentives for LNG production projects (including incentives for the purchase of process equipment), incentives for the infrastructure that provides them, state funding for developing infrastructure facilities in the context of implementing LNG production projects, and stimulating the development and implementation of domestic equipment for the organization of large-capacity production of liquefied natural gas [42].

All measures are aimed at achieving the target volumes of liquefied natural gas production set in the Energy Strategy of the Russian Federation for the period up to 2035 [48], namely 102.5 million tons (~139.4 billion cubic meters) per year by 2030 and 140 million tons (~190.4 billion cubic meters) per year by 2035.

The Russian Far East, including the eastern part of the Arctic, is considered a potential area for increasing LNG production, which is a strategic opportunity for the development of the Far Eastern Federal District gas industry.

5.4.1.3 ARCTIC POTENTIAL

The predominant development in terms of natural gas production and LNG production was received by the Western Arctic, primarily due to the implementation of large-scale projects by NOVATEK PJSC: Yamal LNG (design capacity 16.5 million tons per year) and Arctic LNG 2 (design capacity 19.8 million tons per year).

However, one of the possible directions in the long term may be in the Eastern Arctic, including the fields of the continental shelf [49]. PJSC Rosneft has a particular long-term interest in this direction, as it has licenses for areas in the waters of the eastern Arctic seas (there are nine areas in the Laptev, East Siberian, and Chukchi Seas) [50].

A sharp increase in demand for LNG by the mid-2030s may lead to the attraction of large investments in additional exploration and deep study of potential gas fields in the Eastern Arctic, as well as justify the effectiveness of new LNG projects in the region [51].

5.4.1.4 INTERNATIONAL COOPERATION AND PROJECTS

The prospects for the development of the fuel and energy complex in the Arctic, including the oil and gas sector, are emphasized by the high concentration of both national [52] and international interests [53]. The complementarity of interests and their long-term nature serve as a stable strategic factor in building mutually beneficial international cooperation on the regional development of the fuel and energy complex and the implementation of relevant international projects [54].

An illustrative example of the Russian-Chinese strategic partnership for the implementation of the project "Polar Silk Road" is the "Belt and Road" initiative [55]. The implementation of the project involves not only creating and operating a reliable and short Asia-Europe maritime transport and logistics route but also developing the infrastructure for the Northern Sea Route, including the port system, as well as implementing joint projects in the energy sector (hydrocarbon production and export, including a number to China) [42]. It should be noted that the Chinese side is actively involved in the implementation of the Yamal LNG project, in addition to providing investment and technical support, including the supply of drilling machines and the construction of transport ships [56].

This strategic experience of cooperation can also be implemented in the development of gas fields in the Eastern Arctic, opening up additional strategic opportunities for the Far Eastern Federal District gas industry.

5.4.2 MAIN RESULTS OF THE ANALYSIS OF STRATEGIC THREATS POTENTIALLY HINDERING THE DEVELOPMENT OF LARGE-SCALE LNG PRODUCTION IN THE RUSSIAN FAR EAST

5.4.2.1 INCREASING COMPETITION FROM LNG PRODUCING COUNTRIES

The rapid growth of energy demand in the Asia-Pacific region and the simultaneous transformation in favor of "clean" energy sources increase the attractiveness of the region for countries producing liquefied natural gas. Thus, from 2010 to 2020, not only new participants appeared in the LNG market in the Asia-Pacific region (Papua New Guinea and Angola, for example), but also the leading gas suppliers changed, including Australia (31% of the total market), Qatar (21%), and Malaysia (9.6%) (Tables 5.9 and 5.10).

In the medium term, Russia's main competitors will be the United States, which is designing new production facilities to increase liquefied LNG production by 35.1 million tons (~47.7 billion cubic meters) by 2025, and Qatar, which plans to launch a large-scale liquefaction project with a production capacity of 32 million tons (~43.5 billion cubic meters) in 2025.

TABLE 5.9 Country Structure of LNG Exports to the Asia-Pacific Region in 2010 and 2020 (bcm)

	US	Peru	Trinidad and Tobago	Russian Federation	Oman	Qatar	UAE	Algeria	Angola	Egypt	Nigeria	Australia	Brunei	Indonesia	Malaysia	Papua New Guinea
								2020								
China	4.4	1.5	0.3	6.9	1.4	11.2	0.4	0.2	0.5	0.2	3.3	40.6	1.0	7.4	8.3	4.1
India	3.3	–	0.7	0.7	1.8	14.1	4.8	0.3	3.1	0.2	4.0	1.4	0.1	–	–	–
Japan	6.4	0.9	–	8.4	3.3	11.9	1.4	–	–	0.1	1.9	39.7	5.4	3.0	14.8	4.7
Malaysia	–	–	–	–	–	–	–	–	–	–	0.1	2.6	1.0	–	–	–
Pakistan	1.0	–	–	0.2	0.2	7.1	0.5	0.4	0.1	0.4	0.6	–	–	0.1	0.1	–
Singapore	0.8	–	0.1	0.1	0.2	0.5	–	–	0.3	0.1	–	3.2	0.1	0.4	–	–
South Korea	8.0	2.2	0.1	2.8	5.4	13.0	0.3	–	0.5	0.1	0.5	10.9	0.4	3.7	6.7	0.4
Taiwan	1.5	–	0.2	3.3	0.1	6.9	0.3	–	–	0.2	0.5	6.7	0.3	1.6	1.0	2.2
Thailand	0.7	–	0.2	–	0.2	3.0	–	–	–	0.1	0.3	1.1	0.2	0.3	1.3	0.1
Other Asia Pacific	0.4	–	–	0.1	–	4.1	–	0.1	–	–	0.8	–	–	–	0.6	–
Asia Pacific	26.4	4.6	1.5	22.5	12.7	71.8	7.6	0.9	4.4	1.3	11.9	106.0	8.4	16.4	32.8	11.5

Source: Compiled by the author based on the BP database.

TABLE 5.10 Country Structure of LNG Exports to the Asia-Pacific Region in 2010 and 2020 (bcm) (Continuation)

	US	Peru	Trinidad and Tobago	Russian Federation	Oman	Qatar	UAE	Algeria	Angola	Egypt	Nigeria	Australia	Brunei	Indonesia	Malaysia	Papua New Guinea
								2010								
China	0.85	0.08	0.07	0.51	–	1.61	0.08	–	–	0.08	0.17	5.21	–	2.45	1.68	–
India	–	–	0.66	–	–	10.53	–	–	–	0.09	0.33	–	–	–	–	–
Japan	–	–	0.15	8.23	3.8	10.15	6.96	0.08	–	0.57	0.84	17.66	7.79	17	18.55	
Malaysia	–	–	–	–	–	–	–	–	–	–	–	–	–	–	–	–
Pakistan	–	–	–	–	–	–	–	–	–	–	–	–	–	–	–	–
Singapore	–	–	–	–	–	–	–	–	–	–	–	–	–	–	–	–
South Korea	0.35	0.08	0.88	3.9	6.11	10.16	0.25	–	–	0.98	1.18	1.33	1.05	7.42	6.39	–
Taiwan	–	–	0.51	0.07	0.5	3.75	0.42	–	–	0.17	1.09	1.06	–	2.62	3.8	–
Thailand	–	–	–	–	–	–	–	–	–	–	–	–	–	–	–	–
Other Asia Pacific	–	–	–	–	–	–	–	–	–	–	–	–	–	–	–	–
Asia Pacific	1.2	0.16	2.27	12.71	10.41	36.2	7.71	0.08	0	1.89	3.61	25.26	8.84	29.49	30.42	0

Source: Compiled by the author based on the BP database.

Mozambique, Canada, and Nigeria can also be considered among potential competitors to Russian LNG, whose total production of liquefied gas by 2025 will be about 38.28 million tons (~52 billion cubic meters) [57].

It is predicted that American and Middle Eastern LNG will be a key competitor to Russian liquefied gas in the Asia-Pacific region in the 2030–2040s [45].

5.4.2.2 SANCTIONS POLICY AND TECHNOLOGICAL RESTRICTIONS

One of the significant strategic threats potentially hindering the development of this direction may be the strengthening of the sanctions policy against the Russian oil and gas sector, primarily against domestic companies and their foreign partners focused on implementing joint projects for the extraction of natural gas and the production of liquefied natural gas in the most difficult climatic and geological conditions. All this is reinforced by the lack of highly efficient domestic technologies and equipment for gas liquefaction in large volumes [58].

Thus, already designed LNG plants, for example, the Arctic LNG-2 project of PJSC NOVATEK (Table 5.11), and potentially new ones, including in the Russian Far East and the eastern part of the Russian Arctic Zone, may be under threat to some extent.

TABLE 5.11 NOVATEK's Implementation Plan for the Arctic LNG-2 Project

Project	Commissioning	Design Capacity (million tons)	Owner	Liquefaction Technology
Arctic LNG 2 T1	2022	6.6	Novatek*; CNOOC; CNPC; Total; JOGMEC; Mitsui	Linde LIMUM
Arctic LNG 2 T2	2024	6.6	Novatek*; CNOOC; CNPC; Total; JOGMEC; Mitsui	Linde MFC
Arctic LNG 2 T3	2026	6.6	Novatek*; CNOOC; CNPC; Total; JOGMEC; Mitsui	Linde MFC

Source: World LNG Report (2021); IGU.

5.4.2.3 ALTERNATIVE ENERGY SOURCES AND DOMESTIC ENERGY RESOURCES BASE

Another potential threat to the development of this direction in the Russian Far East should also be considered—a possible drop in demand for natural gas and, accordingly, LNG. On the one hand, this may be due to the Asia-Pacific countries' substitution in their energy balances for energy volumes obtained from fossil energy sources (oil, coal, and gas); on the other hand, due to realizing the possibility of replacing hydrocarbon imports through the development of a domestic resource base [42].

Meanwhile, with regard to the first point, it is worth noting that both with the full implementation of all measures or policies (net zero scenario), in accordance with the Paris Agreement, and with the current course maintained (business-as-usual scenario), including the priority ensuring the energy security of countries, it is assumed that alternative sources (nuclear power and hydro energy, as well as renewable energy sources) will not have a significant impact on the growth in demand for natural gas as an energy source (Figure 5.6).

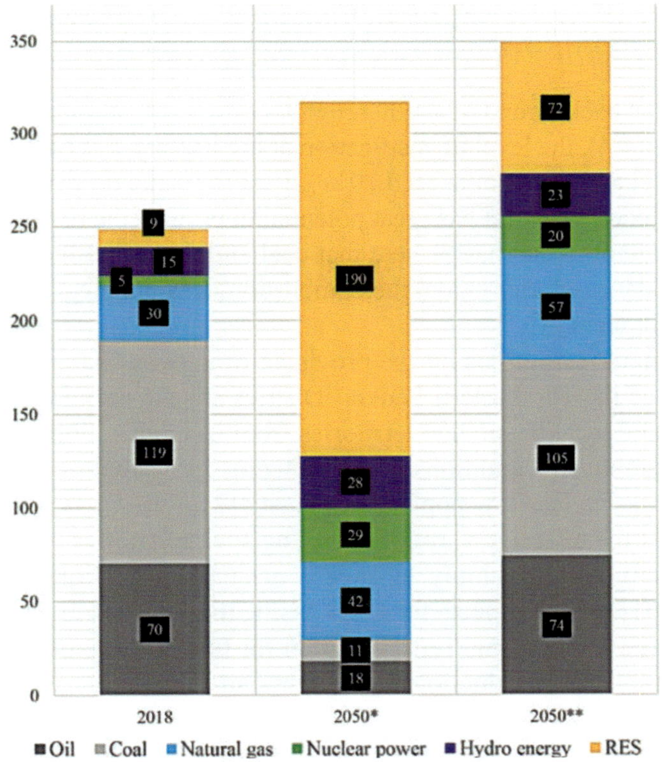

FIGURE 5.6 Forecast values of energy consumption in the Asia-Pacific region energy balance (exajoules).

Note: *net-zero scenario; and **business-as-usual scenario.

Source: Compiled by the author based on BP's "Energy Outlook: 2020 Edition."

The possibility of replacing hydrocarbon imports by developing a domestic resource base is marked by a more significant threat to LNG in the Asia-Pacific region's energy market. This is due to the potential development of both traditional sources of natural gas (~16.6 trillion cubic meters of proven reserves in the Asia-Pacific region in 2020 [32]), and unconventional, primarily shale gas [21] and gas hydrates [40].

5.4.3 MAIN RESULTS OF THE ANALYSIS OF STRATEGIC OPPORTUNITIES THAT JUSTIFY THE DEVELOPMENT OF SMALL-SCALE LNG PRODUCTION IN THE RUSSIAN FAR EAST

5.4.3.1 THE POTENTIAL OF AUTONOMOUS GAS SUPPLY TO THE REGIONS OF THE FAR EASTERN FEDERAL DISTRICT

Against the background of a rather high level of gasification of Russia as a whole (71.4%), the level of gasification of the Russian Far East remains at a low level and does not exceed 20% [2]. At the same time, while the Far Eastern Federal District has great potential to provide the region with gas, it is important to emphasize here that coal and fuel oil still dominate the energy balance of the region, the combustion of which negatively affects the environment [3].

The main restrictions on the provision of network natural gas to the subjects of the Far Eastern Federal District are the remoteness of non-gasified and weakly gasified territories from gas fields, difficult climatic and geographical conditions for organizing gas supplies through gas pipelines, as well as low population density [21, 59].

One of the effective ways of gasifying such territories is determined by autonomous gas supply by means of small-scale liquefied natural gas [60, 61]. The prospects for LNG gasification of the Far East are also emphasized in the Long-Term Program for the Development of Liquefied Natural Gas Production in the Russian Federation. According to estimates, it is the Russian Far East that by 2035 will become the main consumer of small-scale liquefied gas for gas supply purposes (54–55% of total Russian demand) (Table 5.12).

TABLE 5.12 Estimated Demand for Small-Tonnage LNG to Gasify Russia and the Far Eastern Federal District (bcm)

Region	2024		2035	
	Low Scenario	High Scenario	Low Scenario	High Scenario
Russian Federation	2.3	4.2	7.4	9.8
Far Eastern Federal District	0.46	1.21	3.98	5.35
Kamchatka Krai	0.4	0.62	0.66	0.83
Sakhalin region	0.05	0.14	0.15	0.19
Amur region	–	–	0.02	0.02
Primorsky Krai	–	–	1.66	2.07
Khabarovsk Krai	–	–	0.58	0.71
The Republic of Sakha (Yakutia)	0.01	0.46	0.92	1.53

Source: Compiled by the author based on "Long-term Program for the Development of Liquefied Natural Gas Production in the Russian Federation."

In addition to the above calculations on the estimated demand of a number of Far Eastern Federal District subjects for small-scale liquefied natural gas for gas supply purposes, it should be noted that the Republic of Buryatia, Zabaykalsky Krai, and the Chukotka Autonomous Region can also become demand drivers for LNG [62, 63].

It is believed that the use of liquefied natural gas in the Far Eastern Federal District will significantly reduce pollutant emissions [64], increase energy efficiency [65], and ensure the implementation of the national goal of improving the level and quality of life of the population [66].

5.4.3.2 MARITIME FUEL

Maritime transport is of high strategic importance for the Russian Far East as it ensures the effective functioning of transport corridors passing through the territory of the macro-region [67], including the Northern Sea Transport Corridor being formed on the basis of the Northern Sea Route (NSR) [68]. It is believed that the NSR will become a driver direction for increasing cargo traffic in the Russian Far East. According to forecast estimates, taking into account established year-round navigation, the cargo flow along the Northern Sea Route will exceed 150 million tons per year by 2030 (for 2020–32.97 million tons), and by 2035 it will reach 160 million tons [69].

Meanwhile, the global trend in climate change also determines measures to protect the marine environment, primarily related to shipping. Therefore, in 2020, in four emission control zones including the Baltic and the North Seas, restrictions on the sulfur content in marine fuel oil were introduced (no more than 0.1–0.5% of the proportion of sulfur in fuel, depending on the zone) [70]. A similar approach is observed in China, where regulations restrict operation in coastal national emission control zones for ships fueled with fuels containing more than 0.5% sulfur and in inland waters emission control zones for ships with fuels containing more than 0.1% sulfur. It is noted that by 2025 a limit of 0.1% of the proportion of sulfur in fuel can be adopted for all without the exception of China's water emission control zones [71].

The introduction of regulations facilitates the transition of ships from conventional fuels to meeting the requirements. Among the promising types of fuel is liquefied natural gas [72], as it is believed that the conversion of maritime transport to LNG will reduce carbon dioxide emissions by 26%, nitrogen oxides by 94%, and sulfur oxides and soot by 100% [73].

According to forecasts, the number of LNG-powered ships in the world will exceed 2,000 by 2025 [74], and 3,700 units by 2030 [75]. In Russia, an LNG fleet capable of sailing along the Northern Sea Route is already being formed, as Sovcomflot and NOVATEK are implementing a number of large-scale projects for the construction of ice-class gas tankers that will use LNG as maritime fuel [76]. The transition of the Far Eastern maritime transport to liquefied natural gas is also receiving significant support, as PJSC Sberbank plans to invest about 10 billion rubles in the implementation of a project to develop the LNG bunkering infrastructure in the Far Eastern Federal District and to purchase liquefied natural gas bunkering ships (fueled gas) [77].

Thus, given the high potential for the long-term development of the Northern Sea Route and environmental restrictions, especially in the northern waters, the implementation of a strategic opportunity to use liquefied natural gas as a marine fuel is increasingly justified. In the long term, this may become one of the driving directions of the Far Eastern Federal District gas industry [42].

5.4.3.3 NATURAL GAS VEHICLE FUEL

The prospects and significance of the use of liquefied natural gas as a natural gas vehicle fuel (NGV fuel) is substantiated as one of the strategic directions of Russia [77]. According to forecasts, about 30 thousand units of vehicles powered by LNG are expected by 2030 (an increase of more than seven times by 2020), which will reduce annual carbon dioxide emissions by more than 1.5 million tons [78].

NGV fuel has a number of significant advantages compared to traditional fuel, including those that allow reducing carbon dioxide and carbon monoxide emissions by 31% and 36%, respectively, and nitrogen oxide emissions by 11 times (compared to diesel engines). At the same time, it is noted that liquefied natural gas has even more advantages in relation to compressed natural gas, which justifies the need to transfer vehicles specifically to LNG [60].

The use of LNG as a motor fuel is a significant strategic opportunity for the Russian Far East [79]. The Far Eastern Federal District already has a significant potential for the conversion of motor vehicles to NGV fuel, primarily liquefied natural gas (Table 5.13).

TABLE 5.13 Availability of Vehicles with the Ability to Use Natural Gas as a Motor Fuel in the Russian Federation and the Far Eastern Federal District for 2020 (in Units)

Region	Total	CNG	LNG
	Light Vehicle		
Russian Federation	49,259,028	1,18,268	8,94,649
Far Eastern Federal District	2,854,425	8,662	82,801
	Trucks		
Russian Federation	6,564,385	66,625	2,88,318
Far Eastern Federal District	4,73,766	5,925	15,573
	Buses		
Russian Federation	8,50,098	23,153	46,552
Far Eastern Federal District	66,342	977	2,324

Source: Compiled by the author based on the Federal State Statistics Service.

It should be noted that in a number of subjects of the Far Eastern Federal District, active work is underway to transfer vehicles to LNG, among them the Republic of Sakha (Yakutia) [86] and the Kamchatka Krai [81].

In addition to the transfer of vehicles to liquefied natural gas, the possibility of using LNG in railway transport is being considered [82]. Among the main advantages are the high mobility of gas-powered locomotives, as well as the reduction of nitrogen emissions by up to 93% and smoke by up to 85% [83]. Given the plans and programs for developing the transport system, including railway communication in the Russian Far East [84], as well as the planned increase in demand for rail transportation in the macro-region [85], the possibility of using liquefied natural gas as a fuel in rail transport may become of particular relevance in the medium term [42].

5.4.4 MAIN RESULTS OF AN ANALYSIS OF STRATEGIC THREATS THAT POTENTIALLY HINDER DEVELOPING SMALL-SCALE LNG PRODUCTION IN THE RUSSIAN FAR EAST

5.4.4.1 COMPETITION FROM ALTERNATIVE ENERGY SOURCES

One of the threats to achieving the strategic possibility of using small-scale liquefied gas for autonomous gas supply in the Russian Far East is associated with the development of alternative energy sources.

Thus, for the autonomous supply of energy to logistically isolated territories, the question of the advisability of switching to renewable energy sources is increasingly being raised [85]. Meanwhile, it is also noted that in the near future, it will be impossible to achieve a complete replacement of traditional sources, and the maximum share of guaranteed energy supply to remote areas through renewable energy sources may not exceed 30-40%. If we turn to the energy balance of the Russian Far East, we can see that the share of renewable energy sources for 2020 did not exceed 0.01% [3], which does not allow us to consider RES as a significant threat to the use of LNG for the autonomous gas supply of certain Far Eastern Federal District territories, at least in the short and medium term.

The most significant strategic threat to the strategic opportunity for using liquefied natural gas in the autonomous gas supply may be nuclear energy. Thus, it is planned to launch the first pilot project for a low-power nuclear plant in the Republic of Sakha (Yakutia) by 2028 [93], and the possibility of building a nuclear power plant in Primorsky Krai is also being considered [94]. However, given the high mobility of LNG, this threat may not affect the overall volume of liquefied natural gas consumption but only change the end consumer [42].

5.4.4.2 *HYDROGEN ENERGY*

A significant threat to small-scale liquefied natural gas in all of the above areas of use is hydrogen energy. Given the high energy intensity and environmental friendliness, hydrogen is considered the energy of the future, capable of acting as an energy source for the autonomous supply of isolated territories, as well as an energy carrier for marine and motor transport [89].

Based on forecasts, it is estimated that by 2050 hydrogen will take about 18% of the global energy balance, and the annual world consumption of hydrogen will increase to 370 million tons (75 million tons in 2020) [90].

In Russia, the development of hydrogen energy is singled out as one of the directions in the "Energy Strategy of the Russian Federation for the Period Up to 2035" [48]. In addition, an action plan ("road map") for the development of hydrogen energy in the Russian Federation until 2024 was approved [91], in accordance with which about twenty projects are already being developed, and the total investment will amount to 9 billion rubles [92].

KEYWORDS

- **environmental request**
- **gas chemistry**
- **gasification**
- **petrochemical products**
- **Russian Far East regions**
- **strategic direction**
- **strategic threats**

REFERENCES

1. Sasaev, N. I., (2021). Strategic diagnostics at the Russian Far East gas industry. *Russian Journal of Industrial Economics*, *14*(4), 355–368.
2. *By 2026, 35 Regions of the Russian Federation Will Be Fully Gasified*, (2021). RG.ru. https://rg.ru/2021/09/02/reg-dfo/k-2026-godu-budut-polnostiu-gazificirovany-36-regionov-rf.html (accessed on 3 January 2023).
3. *How the Russian Energy Balance Works*, (2021). RG.ru. https://rg.ru/2021/03/28/kak-ustroen-rossijskij-energeticheskij-balans.html (accessed on 3 January 2023).
4. Tarasov, O. V., (2020). *Infrastructure of Spatial Development of the Russian Federation: Transport, Energy, Innovative System, Life Support*. IEIE SB RAS.
5. *The Government Approved the Strategy for the Socio-economic Development of Russia with Low Greenhouse Gas Emissions Until 2050*, (2021). Government.ru. http://government.ru/news/43708 (accessed on 3 January 2023).
6. Vladimir, L. K., & Vyacheslav, A. F., (2021). *The Fundamentals of Russia's Environmental Development Strategy*. Moscow University Press.
7. *Far Eastern Federal District (FEFD).* Council.gov.ru. http://council.gov.ru/services/reference/10483 (accessed on 3 January 2023).
8. Sasaev, N. I., (2022). Strategic opportunities of the Russian Far East gas industry development: Gasification, gas processing, and gas chemistry. *Strategizing: Theory and Practice*, *2*(1), 106–118.
9. Naumov, Yu. A., (2020). On the features of air pollution in the Russian Far East. *Ojkumena. Regional Researches, 1*, 41–52.
10. *Name the Cities of Russia with the Most Polluted Air*, (2021). Lenta.ru. https://lenta.ru/news/2021/12/23/polluted_air (accessed on 3 January 2023).
11. *How Are Things with Air Purity in the Cities of the Far Eastern Federal District*, (2021). RG.ru. https://rg.ru/2021/01/28/reg-dfo/kak-v-gorodah-dfo-obstoiat-dela-s-chistotoj-vozduha.html (accessed on 3 January 2023).
12. *Russia Seeks Leadership in the Global Helium Market*. URL.: http://rcc.ru/article/rossiya-stremitsya-k-liderstvu-na-globalnom-rynke-geliya-81000 (accessed on 3 January 2023).
13. *Gazprom Launched the World's Largest Helium Plant*. URL.: https://www.vedomosti.ru/business/articles/2021/06/10/873639-gazprom-geliya (accessed on 3 January 2023).
14. *Russian Helium Will Fill the Deficit in the World Market*. URL.: https://rg.ru/2021/09/02/rossijskij-gelij-vospolnit-deficit-na-mirovom-rynke.html (accessed on 3 January 2023).
15. *Global Helium Market Update: Market Shifting to Oversupply by mid2020s*. URL.: https://www.edisongroup.com/sector-report/global-helium-market-update-market-shifting-to-oversupply-by-mid-2020s/29444 (accessed on 3 January 2023).
16. *World Helium Market*. URL.: https://gazprom-helium.ru/?id=24 (accessed on 3 January 2023).
17. *Amur Gas Processing Plant*. Gazprom. https://www.gazprom.ru/projects/amur-gpp (accessed on 3 January 2023).

18. *Strategy for the Development of the Chemical and Petrochemical Complex for the Period Up to 2030.* https://docs.cntd.ru/ (accessed on 3 January 2023).
19. *Russia May Triple Polymer Production by 2030*, (2021). Nangs.org. https://nangs.org/news/downstream/rossiya-k-2030-godu-mozhet-utroit-vypusk-polimerov (accessed on 3 January 2023).
20. *The State of Gas Chemistry: The Energy Crisis Is Not a Hindrance—There Will Be Problems, But Not for Everyone*, (2021). Oilcapital.ru. https://oilcapital.ru/news/2021-10-15/sostoyanie-gazohimii-energokrizis-ne-pomeha-problemy-budut-no-ne-u-vseh-1043132 (accessed on 18 January 2024).
21. Filimonova, I. V., Shumilova, S. I., & Dzyuba, Yu. A. Comprehensive analysis and forecast of subsoil use in the regions of eastern Siberia and the Far East. *Ecological Bulletin of Russia*, *10*, 20–27.
22. Sasaev, *Theoretical Foundations and Methodology of the Russian Gas Industry Development Strategy*.
23. Vyatkin, Yu. L., Lishchiner, I. I., Sinitsyn, S. A., & Kuzmin, A. M., (2020). *Prospective Directions of Chemical Processing of Hydrocarbon Raw Materials* (Vol. 4, No.100, pp. 114–118). Neftegaz.ru.
24. *Russia May Increase the Export of Polyolefins by 10 Times by 2030,* (2020). Agusmedia.com. https://www.argusmedia.com/ru/news/2146773-rossiia-mozhet-narastit-eksport-poliolefinov-v-10-raz-k-2030-g (accessed on 3 January 2023).
25. *Amur Gas Chemical Complex.* URL: https://amur-gcc.ru/ (accessed on 18 January 2024).
26. Kalinenko, E. A., (2021). *Review of the Petrochemical Industry in Russia* (Vol. 1, No. 109, pp. 70–78). Neftegaz.ru.
27. Braginskiy, O. B., (2021). Russian petrochemical industry: A new road. *Oil &Gas Chemistry, 3, 4*, 5–8.
28. Polymer Market to Hit $838.5 Billion Revenue by 2030: P&S Intelligence, (202[illegible]) https://www.prnewswire.com/news-releases/polymer-market-to-hit-838-5-billion-revenue-by-2030-ps-intelligence-301229622.html (accessed on 18 January 2024).
29. *Global Polyethylene Industry Outlook to 2024 – Capacity and Capital Expenditure Forecasts with Details of All Active and Planned Plants*, (2020). Global Data. https://store.globaldata.com/report/global-polyethylene-industry-outlook-to-2024-capacity-and-capital-expenditure-forecasts-with-details-of-all-active-and-planned-plants (accessed on 3 January 2023).
30. *Global Polypropylene Industry Outlook to 2025–Capacity and Capital Expenditure Forecasts with Details of All Active and Planned Plants*, (2023). Global Data. https://store.globaldata.com/report/global-polypropylene-industry-outlook-to-2025-capacity-and-capital-expenditure-forecasts-with-details-of-all-active-and-planned-plants (accessed on 3 January 2023).
31. Sasaev, N. I., (2022). Network gas export is a strategic priority of the gas industry of the Russian Far East. *Russian Journal of Industrial Economics*, *15*(1), 17–25.
32. *BP's Statistical Review of World Energy,* (2021). BP, https://www.bp.com/en/global/corporate/energy-economics/statistical-review-of-world-energy.html (accessed on 3 January 2023).

33. *Energy Outlook: 2020 Edition.* BP. https://www.bp.com/content/dam/bp/business-sites/en/global/corporate/pdfs/energy-economics/energy-outlook/bp-energy-outlook-2020.pdf (accessed on 3 January 2023).
34. *World Energy Outlook,* (2021). IEA, https://www.iea.org/reports/world-energy-outlook-2021/executive-summary (accessed on 3 January 2023).
35. Ibid.
36. *The Fourteenth Five-Year Plan for the National Economic and Social Development of the People's Republic of China and the Outline of the Long-term Goals for 2035*, (2021). Gov.cn. http://www.gov.cn/xinwen/2021–03/13/content_5592681.htm (accessed on 3 January 2023).
37. *India's Greenhouse Gas Policy Is Driven by the Paris Agreement*, (2021). NG.ru., https://www.ng.ru/energy/2021-09-13/15_8250_india.html (accessed on 18 January 2024).
38. *Russia and India Will Focus on Cooperation in the Gas Sector*, (2021). RG.ru. https://rg.ru/2021/03/02/rossiia-i-indiia-sdelaiut-upor-na-sotrudnichestvo-v-gazovoj-sfere.html (accessed on 3 January 2023).
39. *The Expert Predicts the Growth of Gas Production in the Bay of Bengal,* (2021). 1Prime.ru. https://1prime.ru/gas/20211008/834907858.html (accessed on 3 January 2023).
40. Shakirova, M. V., et al., (2020). Features and methods of investigation of underwater gas-hydrates and their resources in the Seas of East Asia. *Underwater Investigations and Robotics*, *3*(33), 63–71.
41. *Gas Hydrates: Science and Applications.* Kommersant.ru. https://www.kommersant.ru/doc/4750809 (accessed on 3 January 2023).
42. Sasaev, N. I., (2022). Strategic opportunities for LNG production development in the Far East. *The Economic Revival of Russia*, *2*(72), 161–178.
43. *Report Extract 2021–2025: Rebound and Beyond.* IEA.org. https://www.iea.org/reports/gas-2020/2021-2025-rebound-and-beyond (accessed on 18 January 2024).
44. Jaganathan, J., (2021). *LNG Demand to Rise 25–50% by 2030, Fastest Growing Hydrocarbon—Morgan Stanley*. Reuters. https://www.reuters.com/article/asia-lng-idUKL1N2RL0KO (accessed on 3 January 2023).
45. Shell LNG Outlook, (2021). Shell. https://www.shell.com/energy-and-innovation/natural-gas/liquefied-natural-gas-lng/lng-outlook-2021.html#iframe=L3dlYmFwcHMvTE5HX091dGxvb2svMjAyMS8 (accessed on 3 January 2023).
46. Sher, R., et al., (2021). *High LNG Prices Put Spotlight on India's Exposure to Global Gas Market Volatility*. SP Global. https://www.spglobal.com/platts/en/market-insights/latest-news/lng/101521-high-lng-prices-put-spotlight-on-indias-exposure-to-global-gas-market-volatility (accessed on 3 January 2023).
47. *The Government Approved a Long-Term Program for the Development of LNG Production.* Government.ru. http://government.ru (accessed on 3 January 2023).
48. *On Approval of the Energy Strategy of the Russian Federation for the Period Up to 2035*. https://docs.cntd.ru (accessed on 3 January 2023).
49. *A Region with Potential for Oil and Gas Was Found in the Laptev Sea, As in Western Siberia,* (2021). Interfax.ru. https://www.interfax.ru/russia/759570 (accessed on 3 January 2023).

50. *Shelf Projects, PJSC Rosneft*. https://www.rosneft.ru/business/Upstream/offshore/#a2 (accessed on 3 January 2023).
51. *Rosneft Is Interested in Gas Production in the Arctic*, (2020). RBC.ru. https://www.rbc.ru/business/03/06/2020/5ebbc9889a7947eb926732d9 (accessed on 3 January 2023).
52. *On the Strategy for the Development of the Arctic Zone of the Russian Federation and Ensuring National Security for the Period up to 2035*. Kremlin.ru. http://www.kremlin.ru/acts/bank/45972 (accessed on 3 January 2023).
53. Lipina, S. A., Fadeev, A. M., Zaikov, K. S., Lipina, A. V., & Kondratov, N. A., (2021). Current stage of international cooperation in the Arctic: Search for answers to the challenges of economic development. *Economic and Social Changes: Facts, Trends, Forecast*, *14*(4), 251–265.
54. Novikova, E. S., & Kripak, A. V., (2021). Some issues of cooperation between Russia and China in the Arctic. *Izvestiya of Saratov University, Sociology. Politology*, *21*(3), 335–339.
55. Kolzina, A. L., & Mindubaeva, A. A., (2020). The Polar Silk Road as a sphere of strategic partnership between the Russian Federation and China. *Bulletin of Udmurt University, Sociology; Political Science; International Relations*, *T4*(2), 186–195.
56. Mikhaylichenko, K. M., (2019). The project "Ice Silk Road" within the framework of the initiative "One Belt and one road" is the realization of the interests of Russia and China in the Arctic region. *RUDN Journal of Political Science, 21*(2), 333–345.
57. *World LNG Report 2021*. IGU. https://www.igu.org/resources/world-lng-report-2021 (accessed on 3 January 2023).
58. Gimaeva, A. R., & Khasanov, I. I., (2021). Analysis of modern Russian and foreign technologies for producing liquefied natural gas in arctic conditions. *Oil & Gas Chemistry*, *1*, *2*, 33–36.
59. Ditriev, A. I., (2010). JSC "Gazprom Gazenergoset" and the prospects for the development of autonomous gasification of the regions of Siberia and the Far East. *Gas Industry*, *S14*(654), 63–66.
60. Sasaev, N. I., (2019). The strategic opportunities of the development of small-scale production of LNG in Russia. *Russian Journal of Industrial Economics*, *12*(2), 136–146.
61. *Prospects for LNG Gasification in the Far East*. NGV.ru, http://www.ngv.ru/magazines/article/perspektivy-spg-gazifikatsii-na-dalnem-vostoke (accessed on 3 January 2023).
62. *Gazprom is Considering the Prospects for Gasification of the Republic of Buryatia and the Zabaykalsky Krai*. Neftegaz, https://neftegaz.ru/news/gazoraspredelenie/676417-gazprom-rassmatrivaet-perspektivy-gazifikatsii-respubliki-buryatiya-i-zabaykalskogo-kraya (accessed on 3 January 2023).
63. *Chukotka Believes that the Use of LNG in the Region Will Facilitate Navigation Along the Northern Sea Route*. Neftegaz, https://neftegaz.ru/news/spg-szhizhennyy-prirodnyy-gaz/532057-na-chukotke-schitayut-chto-ispolzovanie-spg-v-regione-budet-sposobstvovat-sudokhodstvu-po-sevmorputi (accessed on 3 January 2023).
64. *The Russian Far East—New Challenges and Opportunities. Improving the Return on Oil and Gas for Russians*. ForumVostok. https://forumvostok.ru/news/

dalnij-vostok-novye-vyzovy-i-vozmozhnosti-povyshenie-otdachi-ot-nefti-i-gaza-dlja-rossijan-1/ (accessed on 18 January 2024).
65. Demina, O. V., & Dzhurka, N. G., (2020). Assessing the economic consequences of reducing emissions in the power supply system of the region: The experience of the Far East. *Regionalistika [Regionalistics]*, *7*(2), 5–23.
66. *Decree of the President of the Russian Federation No. 400 "On the National Security Strategy of the Russian Federation*, (2021). http://publication.pravo.gov.ru (accessed on 3 January 2023).
67. *The Exclusive Role of Maritime Transport in the Russian Far East*. Marketing RBC, https://marketing.rbc.ru/articles/280 (accessed on 3 January 2023).
68. *A Year-round Transport Corridor Will Be Created on the Basis of the Northern Sea Route,* (2021). IZ.ru. https://iz.ru/1195308/2021-07-19/na-baze-sevmorputi-sozdadut-kruglogodichnyi-transportnyi-koridor (accessed on 18 January 2024).
69. *"Year-round Northern Sea Route" is Recognized as a Strategic Project of the State*, (2021). Vedomosti. https://www.vedomosti.ru/business/articles/2021/07/25/879485-sevmorput-strategicheskim (accessed on 3 January 2023).
70. Skaridov, A., (2021). "Green shipping" and the problem of sustainable use of maritime Transport. *International Law and International Organizations*, *1*, 31–45.
71. Klimentyev, A., Knizhnikov, A., & Grigoryev, A., (2017). Prospects for the use of LNG in the Arctic region of Russia according to estimates of the Worldwide Fund for nature (WWF). *Oil & Gas Journal Russia*, *5*, 72–78.
72. *LNG Fuel for Ships Is Forced to Be Attractive*, (2021). *Oilcapital.ru*. https://oilcapital.ru/article/general/13–05–2021/spg-toplivo-dlya-sudov-delayut-privlekatelnym-nasilno (accessed on 3 January 2023).
73. *Development of NGV-Fueled Ships*. Morvesti.ru, https://morvesti.ru/analitika/1691/90216/ (accessed on 18 January 2024).
74. *The Expert Spoke About the Creation of an LNG "Fleet" in Russia*. Krylov Centre, https://krylov-centre.ru/press/press-about-ksrc/1418 (accessed on 3 January 2023).
75. *LNG Carriers—The Rapid Development of the Industry*, (2021). CDU.ru. https://www.cdu.ru/tek_russia/articles/3/944 (accessed on 3 January 2023).
76. *Sberbank Will Invest More than 10 Billion Rubles in the Conversion of the Far Eastern Maritime Transport to LNG*, (2021). Interfax.ru. https://www.interfax.ru/business/788331 (accessed on 3 January 2023).
77. *Mikhail Mishustin Approved the Road Map for the Development of the Small-Tonnage LNG and Gas Motor Fuel Market Until 2025*. Government.ru. http://government.ru/news/41564 (accessed on 3 January 2023).
78. Nikolai, S. (2021). *"Methane Consumption in the Form of GMT Will Increase by 25–30% by the End of 2021."* https://sro150.ru/novosti/4157-08-10-2021-nikolaj-shulginov-potreblenie-metana-v-vide-gmt-vyrastet-k-kontsu-2021-goda-na-25-30 (accessed on 18 January 2024).
79. *The Development of the Gas Motor Fuel Market Will Stimulate the Economy of the Far Eastern Regions*. Minvr.gov.ru. http://assoc.khv.gov.ru/news/3857 (accessed on 18 January 2024).
80. *Yakutia Switches to LNG,* (2021). Vnedra.ru. https://www.vnedra.ru/lyudi/intervyu/yakutiya-perehodit-na-spg-14490 (accessed on 3 January 2023).

81. *The Authorities of Kamchatka are Planning to Transfer the Fleet of Regional Enterprises to Gas Motor Fuel*, (2020). Interfax Russia. https://www.interfax-russia.ru/far-east/news/vlasti-kamchatki-planiruyut-perevesti-avtopark-kraevyh-predpriyatiy-na-gazomotornoe-toplivo (accessed on 3 January 2023).
82. *The Introduction of Gas Motor Fuel in Transport Promises Benefits*, (2020). RG.ru. https://rg.ru/2020/09/03/za-chetyre-goda-chislo-avtomobilej-na-gmt-v-rossii-vyrastet-v-4-raza.html (accessed on 3 January 2023).
83. *Natural Gas on the Railway: A Promising Type of Fuel?* RZD-Partner.ru. https://www.rzd-partner.ru/zhd-transport/comments/prirodnyy-gaz-na-zheleznoy-doroge-perspektivnyy-vid-topliva (accessed on 3 January 2023).
84. *On Approval of the State Program of the Russian Federation "Development of the Transport System."* https://docs.cntd.ru/document/556157375 (accessed on 3 January 2023).
85. *The Development of Transport Accessibility in the Far East Was Discussed by the Participants of the Round Table in Preparation for the EEF 2021*, Minvr.ru. https://minvr.gov.ru/press-center/news/3235 (accessed on 3 January 2023).
86. *The Groundwork for the Development of Renewable Energy Has Already Been Formed in the Far East and the North*, (2021). Nangs.org. https://nangs.org/news/renewables/zadel-dlya-razvitiya-vie-uzhe-sformirovan-na-dalnem-vostoke-i-severe (accessed on 3 January 2023).
87. *By 2028, a Low-power Nuclear Power Plant will be Built in Yakutia*. Rosatom. https://rosatom.ru/journalist/news/k-2028-godu-v-yakutii-budet-postroena-atomnaya-stantsiya-maloy-moshchnosti (accessed on 3 January 2023).
88. *Nuclear Power Plant is Planned to be Built in Primorye*, (2021). EastRussia. https://www.eastrussia.ru/news/atomnuyu-es-planiruyut-postroit-v-primore (accessed on 3 January 2023).
89. Novak, A., (2021). Hydrogen: The energy of a "clean" future. *Energy Policy, 4*(158), 6–11.
90. Hydrogen energy: how widely, how soon. (2021). https://energypolicy.ru/vodorodnaya-energetika-kak-shiroko-kak-skoro/energoperehod/2021/12/22/ (accessed on 18 January 2024).
91. Vechkinzova, E., Steblyakova, L. P., Roslyakova, N., & Omarova, B. (2022). Prospects for the Development of Hydrogen Energy: Overview of Global Trends and the Russian Market State. *Energies, 15*(22), 8503.
92. *Nine Billion Rubles Will Be Allocated for the Development of Hydrogen Energy in Russia Over Three Years*, (2021). Vedomosti. https://www.vedomosti.ru/economics/news/2021/10/15/891512-novak-rasskazal-o-mezhdunarodnom-sotrudnichestve (accessed on 3 January 2023).

CHAPTER 6

The Concept of the Russian Far East Gas Industry Strategy

6.1 FORMATION OF THE STRATEGY MISSION CONCEPT

The gas industry is of particular strategic importance for the development of all subjects of the Russian Far East as a macro-region, which consists, first of all, of the reliable supply of households and industry with efficient and environmentally friendly energy resources [1].

The results of strategic diagnostics show that the gas industry of the Far Eastern Federal District has a high accumulated scientific, technical, resource, industrial, and production development potential [2]. Three large gas production centers (Yakutia, Sakhalin, and Kamchatsky) are localized in the Russian Far East, including fields on land and offshore, with a total concentration of more than 5 trillion cubic meters of natural gas reserves.

In the long term, an increase in resource opportunities is expected due to the intensification of geological exploration [3]. In addition, gas and oil and gas condensate fields of the macro-region have a number of key features, for example, the Chayandinskoye oil and gas condensate field has significant volumes of helium, ethane, propane, and butane, which is an unconditional competitive advantage [1].

Unfavorable climatic conditions and complex mining and geological features of the region have led to a high level of contingency between the development of oil and gas fields and the development and successful implementation of advanced technologies both within the industry and in related areas [4]. The successful experience of such large-scale projects as the subsea high-tech complex for offshore gas production, the Amur Gas Processing Plant, and complexes with low-manned gas production

Strategizing the Russian Gas Industry: The Far Eastern Vector. Nikita I. Sasaev (Ed)

technologies not only confirm the demand for advanced technologies but also act as anchor points for the growth of innovations [5]. An important role in this process is the presence in the region and active participation in the industrial development of leading oil and gas companies, among them [6]: PJSC Gazprom, PJSC YATEK, LLC Taas-Yuryakh Neftegazodobycha, Surgutneftegas PJSC, and PJSC Rosneft.

As shown by the strategic analysis of interests [7], the functioning of the gas industry covers a wide range of interest groups (national, public, regional, industrial, corporate, and international). Both for the population of the regions and for industry, the gas industry is a reliable source of energy resources and domestic gas chemical products [8]. In general, at the level of each of the Far Eastern Federal District subjects, there is a complete conviction that the gas industry can have a tangible positive impact in terms of the socio-economic development of the regions and the Far Eastern Federal District as a whole [7, 9]. In addition to contributing to the implementation of the national goal of improving the population's welfare, the gas industry is seen as one of the significant actors in the environmental development of Russian regions, including the Russian Far East, which implies a significant reduction in emissions of pollutants into the atmosphere in the medium term [10].

In turn, the deep integration of the region into international economic relations, including in the energy sector with Asia-Pacific countries, creates long-term channels for investment and technological cooperation [5].

Based on the entire previous analysis, it is proposed as a mission concept to ensure favorable economic, business, and regulatory conditions for implementing the accumulated scientific, technical, resource, and industrial and production potentials of the Russian Far East gas industry in the context of a multiplicative stimulation of the socio-economic development of each of the Far East Federal District subjects and the macro-region as a whole for the period up to 2035 and beyond.

The formulated mission declares the following general goal, namely the achievement of a multiple improvement in the quality and standard of living of the Russian Far East's population through building an innovative driver for long-term development based on the gas industry.

The uniqueness of the developed gas strategy also lies in the fact that it is designed to unite all Far Eastern Federal District subjects, as well as all interested actors (including potential investors), in the context of achieving the general goal, strengthening vertical and horizontal links in the context of the overall system of strategies, and contributing to the multiplication and scaling of the achieved economic and social effects from implementing strategic opportunities for the development of the Russian Far East gas industry.

6.2 FORMATION OF THE STRATEGY VISION CONCEPT

To ensure the successful fulfillment of the Russian Far East gas industry's mission and general goal, it is necessary to rely on the following system of general methodological and specific strategic principles (Table 6.1).

TABLE 6.1 Strategic Principles of Strategizing the Russian Far East Gas Industry

Strategic Principle	Description
Public utility	The strategy of the Russian Far East gas industry, including all its strategic priorities and decisions, must ultimately be focused on humankind. The primary outcome of the strategy should be public utility.
Interest complementarity	All interest groups, without exception, included in the development stage of the Russian Far East gas industry strategy must be fully implemented. In addition, it is necessary to organize a mechanism to include newly emerging interest groups throughout the strategy during all stages of its implementation.
Hierarchy and integration	Throughout the period being strategized, vertical and horizontal interconnection of the FEFD gas industry with other objects within the general system of strategies (including through federal ministries, regional, and municipal administrations and departments, corporations, and foreign representative offices) should be maintained. To do this, it is necessary to create mechanisms and tools that establish such interaction and contribute to the joint implementation of the general directions of the strategy.
Environmental friendliness	Considering the clear environmental advantages of natural gas over other fossil fuels, the Russian Far East gas industry strategy should contribute to improving the environmental situation in the long term.
Innovation	Priority should be given to strategic opportunities that involve innovative strategic solutions for developing the Far Eastern Federal District gas industry. In this regard, it is necessary to build and operate a strategic system for monitoring and implementing innovations at all stages of strategizing.

TABLE 6.1 *(Continued)*

Strategic Principle	Description
Resource availability	All strategic priorities of the Russian Far East gas industry should be based on specific competitive advantages and have sufficient resources. Resources should be concentrated only on well-founded strategic priorities and decisions, avoiding the "scattering" of the resource base. Additionally, it should be possible to build and operate additional mechanisms and tools to expand resource capabilities throughout the entire strategy period.
Consistency and completeness	It is mandatory to follow the established procedure for the development and implementation of the Russian Far East gas industry strategy, as well as the full implementation of the conceived doctrine.
Efficiency and multiplicativity	The implementation of all strategic priorities of the FEFD gas industry should generate both public and economic (budgetary and commercial) efficiency. Particular attention should be paid to the multiplication and scaling of the resulting effects.

Source: Compiled by the authors [8, 11].

Based on complex strategic analysis [12–14], the concept of the mission, and strategic principles, six concepts of the Russian Far East gas industry's main strategic priorities are formulated, providing for synchronous implementation. Due to the commonality of effects, public and economic efficiency is grouped according to some strategic priorities.

6.2.1 STRATEGIC PRIORITY "EXPORT OF PIPELINE GAS TO THE ASIA-PACIFIC REGION"

The interconnected global trends of "climate change" and "energy market transformation" will ultimately drive a move away from "dirty" energy sources in favor of environmentally friendly ones [13]. This is especially evident in the countries of the Asia-Pacific region, which contribute a significant amount of carbon dioxide emissions (over 52% of the global volume) [14].

The emerging environmental window of opportunity, supported by relevant national strategic documents, primarily in China [15] and India [16] (the largest issuers of the Asia-Pacific region), as well as the existing energy window of opportunity associated with the shift of industrial centers in the Asia-Pacific region and the simultaneous increase in primary energy consumption in rapidly developing Asian countries [14], determines the strategic possibility of a multiple increase in Russian pipeline natural gas exports from the Russian Far East to the markets of the Asia-Pacific region. The most promising market is China, as its projected demand for natural gas in the period up to 2050 will exceed domestic supply by more than 2.1 times [17].

In this regard, the main goal of this priority is the organization of long-term large-scale supplies of pipeline natural gas from the Russian Far East to the Asia-Pacific market. The main resource base of the priority is assumed to be gas and gas condensate fields from the Yakutia gas production center. The undoubted competitive advantage is the strategic proximity of the main gas fields in the Far Eastern Federal District to key external sales markets.

6.2.2 STRATEGIC PRIORITY "DEVELOPMENT OF LARGE-SCALE LNG PRODUCTION IN THE RUSSIAN FAR EAST"

Together with the global trends already mentioned above related to climate change and subsequent energy market transformation, another trend—the "formation of the global natural gas market"—coupled with a rapid increase in demand for liquefied natural gas in interregional trade [13, 18], determines a strategic opportunity to increase LNG production in the Russian Far East on a large scale and expand its exports to the main markets and, first of all, to Asian-Pacific countries. At the national level, this priority is supported by active government incentives and significant support, which provides for a number of tax breaks and incentives aimed at the comprehensive development of LNG projects.

Altogether, this determines the final goal of this priority, namely, building a large cluster for large-scale LNG production and organizing its export to the end consumer in the emerging global natural gas market.

Due to the fact that China (growth by 1.85 times) [19], India (growth by 3.7 times) [20], Taiwan, Thailand, and Bangladesh are predicted to be the main drivers of demand for liquefied natural gas by 2040, it is proposed to focus primarily on this target group, which will allow the full realization of competitive advantage in terms of strategic proximity to key consumers. Another emerging competitive advantage is the developed domestic technology for liquefying natural gas called "Arctic Cascade," which implies a significant reduction in the cost of liquefying gas through the use of arctic climate conditions [21], and which will additionally open up a strategic opportunity to realize the resource potential of the Eastern Arctic. However, first of all, the local reserves of natural gas concentrated in the macro-region including all three gas production centers (Yakutia, Sakhalin, and Kamchatsky) can serve as a resource for the implementation of the priority.

The strategic priorities "Export of Pipeline Gas to the Asia-Pacific Region" and "Development of Large-scale LNG Production in the Russian Far East" provide for the achievement of a number of co-directional effects.

From the standpoint of public efficiency, the implementation of both priorities leads to an increase in natural gas exports, which is seen as an additional incentive for the development of fields in the areas of the main centers of gas production and leads to the expansion of exploration activities to search for new fields throughout the Far Eastern Federal District. In turn, this will affect the growth of relevant production capacities and infrastructure, including main gas pipelines and large-scale LNG plants, stimulating an increase in investment flows to the regions with the creation of new jobs.

Among the main effects on budgetary (state) efficiency, it is envisaged that an increase in export volumes of pipeline and liquefied natural gas will lead to an increase in the tax base and will become one of the significant channels for accumulating federal budget funds and regional budgets funds for the Far Eastern Federal District, which should be directed to the development infrastructure and construction of social facilities in the macro-region.

In addition, the organization of close cooperation between the Far Eastern Federal District, as a gas supplier, and the Asia-Pacific countries, as gas recipients, will positively affect the expansion and strengthening of foreign trade relations with the developing economies of the region, including in the field of interregional cooperation in oil and gas equipment and technologies. Expansion of foreign trade activity will become one of the factors of multiplicative stimulation of economic growth in the Russian Far East and the macro-region as a whole.

As the main effects of commercial efficiency, it is worth highlighting the increase in investment attractiveness in Far Eastern Federal District subjects, associated with the scaling up of work in developing oil and gas fields and building the appropriate infrastructure, which helps to attract significant investment and increase business activity.

6.2.3 STRATEGIC PRIORITY "ENSURING GASIFICATION OF THE RUSSIAN FAR EAST"

The global trend of "energy market transformation" finds support not only at the national [13], but also at the intra-regional level, which opens up a strategic window of opportunity for natural gas in the Russian Far East, and which has a high potential for regional gasification, as well as a corresponding environmental demand (e.g., environmental pollution is an acute problem, both at the regional and municipal levels) [22].

Over 50% of electricity generation in the Russian Far East is generated by thermal power plants, of which about 70% is produced by burning coal [23]. The Far Eastern Federal District is characterized as a macro-region with a rather low overall level of gasification (~20% at the end of 2021) and in some Far Eastern Federal District subjects, the level of gasification is still practically at zero level [12]. Considering this, the organization of reliable and uninterrupted gas supply to the population and industry of the Far Eastern Federal District subjects in optimal volumes is necessary. A significant increase in the level of gasification of Far Eastern Federal District subjects by 2035 is set as the overall resulting goal.

Due to the climatic and relief features of the macro-region, the gasification of Far Eastern Federal District subjects can be carried out in two directions: network and autonomous gas supply.

6.2.4 STRATEGIC PRIORITY "DEVELOPMENT OF SMALL-SCALE LNG PRODUCTION IN THE RUSSIAN FAR EAST"

Small-scale liquefied natural gas is considered as one of the promising energy sources in the context of a comprehensive solution to the issues of ensuring energy efficiency and environmental friendly fuel [8]. Therefore, in the Russian Far East, there are three main strategic opportunities for the use of small-scale LNG.

First of all, it is important to note the high potential of using small-scale liquefied natural gas for the purpose of autonomous gas supply to remote gas production sites and hard-to-reach areas with difficult climatic and geographical conditions. It is predicted that the Far Eastern Federal District will become one of the growth drivers in demand for small-scale LNG for the needs of autonomous gas supply (~55% of the total Russian demand) [24] by 2035.

Another strategic opportunity simultaneously relates to the strengthening of regulatory measures for protecting the environment in the waters related to shipping (emission control zones, including the Baltic and North Sea areas and China's national coastal emission control areas) as a response to the global climate change trend [25] and with the active development of the Northern Sea Route, which implies both an increase in the number of ships that meet new environmental requirements and an increase in demand for small-scale LNG as one of the promising and environmentally friendly types of maritime fuel.

Against the backdrop of environmental trends, a no less significant strategic opportunity is the partial transfer of vehicles in the Far Eastern Federal District subject to small-scale LNG as a natural gas vehicle fuel.

In this regard, the main goal of the priority is to create a large-scale system of small-scale liquefied natural gas production in the Far Eastern Federal District and the active use of LNG for autonomous gas supply as maritime and natural gas vehicle fuel.

A clear and priority competitive advantage is the unique technologies available in Russia for small-scale liquefaction of natural gas. Among them is the unique technology of OOO Gazprom Transgaz Yekaterinburg [8], which is successfully implemented on the basis of gas distribution stations (GDS) and automobile compressed natural gas fueling stations (NGV filling stations) [26], which opens up the possibility of placing such small-scale LNG plants at GDS and NGV filling stations in the Far Eastern Federal District.

The strategic priorities "Ensuring Gasification of the Russian Far East" and "Development of Small-scale LNG Production in the Russian Far East" will lead to an increase in the quality and standard of living of the Far Eastern Federal District's population. This is facilitated by two effects [8]: environmental (a significant reduction in emissions of pollutants into the environment [27]) and economic (providing access to an energy resource that has a competitive advantage in terms of energy efficiency/cost to diesel fuel, fuel oil, and coal). In addition, the development of the gas pipeline network, the construction of new GDS and NGV filling stations, small-scale LNG plants, and other infrastructure will provide an increase in new jobs in Far Eastern Federal District subjects.

In the context of budgetary (state) efficiency, improving the environmental situation through gasification of the regions, the use of LNG-powered NGV fuel, as well as greening the energy systems of the Russian Far East, will lead to an increase in the population's quality of life, which is one of the significant factors in shaping the attractiveness of the Far Eastern Federal District and contributes not only to its preservation, but also to population growth. An additional effect of improving the environment is a reduction in the cost required to eliminate damage from negative anthropogenic impacts on the environment.

The use of ecological maritime fuel-LNG in the waters of the Northern Sea Route will ensure growing cargo flows, contributing to the construction of appropriate infrastructure and the development of coastal areas.

In general, due to energy efficiency and the economy, providing the population and industry with natural gas will lead to a multiplied stimulation of economic growth in the subjects of the Far Eastern Federal District [8, 28].

Commercial efficiency, first of all, consists of gaining industry access to a relatively cheap and more efficient source of energy and LNG-powered NGV fuel, which together will reduce costs and improve the energy efficiency of industries and enterprises, ultimately increasing the competitiveness of finished products.

In turn, increasing the attractiveness of the Northern Sea Route through the transition to the use of environmentally friendly LNG maritime fuel will open up new strategic opportunities for increasing business activity in coastal regions.

6.2.5 STRATEGIC PRIORITY "DEVELOPMENT OF GAS PROCESSING AND GAS CHEMICAL PRODUCTION IN THE RUSSIAN FAR EAST"

The growth of the global economy and the regional trend of "industrial center displacement" not only have a stimulating effect on the growth in demand for primary energy in a number of regions globally but also enhance the growth in demand for chemical products and composite materials [13]. It is noted that natural gas is one of the promising sources of raw materials [29], through gas processing and further gas chemistry it is expected to obtain a whole range of highly-processed chemical and gas chemical products.

Based on the fact that the territory of the Far Eastern Federal District contains significant reserves of natural gas with a high content of ethane, butane, propane, and one of the largest reserves of helium in the world (8.3 billion cubic meters or ~50% of Russian reserves) [5], there are a number of relevant strategic opportunities for the integrated development of gas processing and gas chemistry in the Russian Far East. First is the production of helium, the world demand for which will increase by more than 21% in the medium term, as well as the production of highly processed gas chemical products, including the production of polymers of ethylene, propylene, etc. (annual global demand for polymers will be 5.1% through 2030) [12].

The goal of the strategic priority is to form a gas chemical cluster in the Russian Far East, capable of meeting both domestic needs for chemical and gas chemical products in the long term and ensuring Russia's leading position in the global and regional chemical product markets, including the markets of the Asia-Pacific region.

In accordance with the goal and national interests, first of all, the gas chemical cluster of the Far Eastern Federal District is designed to ensure the import substitution of chemical products on the national market, where a significant proportion of dependence on imported products remains [30].

Competitive advantages that ensure the implementation of the strategic priority are the accumulated domestic experience in the field of gas processing and gas chemistry, as well as unique domestic technological and technical developments that are successfully implemented in the relevant industries, for example, at the Amur gas processing and gas chemical complexes [12].

The implementation of large-scale projects for the development of gas processing and gas chemical production in the Russian Far East, on the one hand, will ensure the creation of new jobs for the local population; on the other hand, an increase in the volume of domestic gas chemistry products and the transition of industries and enterprises from imported analogs will increase the availability of these domestic products for the population [13], acting as one of the factors of the multiplier social effect in the development of Far Eastern Federal District subjects.

Within the framework of budgetary (state) efficiency, it is envisaged to achieve the following main effects, which also correspond to the national strategic priority for the development of gas processing and gas chemistry [31]:

- A significant increase in the share of gas processing production and the output of domestic chemical and gas chemical products, which contributes to strengthening the stability of the regional economies of the Far Eastern Federal District and the Russian economy as a whole in relation to external and internal challenges and threats of various nature (economic, energy, political, etc.);
- A general decrease in the import dependence of the national economy due to the saturation of the domestic market with cheap domestic chemical and gas chemical products;
- Strengthening of interregional interaction and economic links between subjects, both within the Far Eastern Federal District and other subjects of the Russian Federation;
- Expansion and strengthening of foreign trade relations by increasing the export of domestic chemical and gas chemical products, primarily with the countries of the Asia-Pacific region;
- Stimulating a multiplier effect on the economic growth of Far Eastern Federal District subjects through the transition to affordable and relatively cheap chemical and gas chemical products.

In addition to increasing investment attractiveness through the implementation of large-scale projects to form a gas chemical cluster in the Russian Far East, the key commercial effect will be the organization of access to cheap raw materials for industries and enterprises, which will open up strategic opportunities for industrial development in the subjects of the Far Eastern Federal District.

6.2.6 STRATEGIC PRIORITY "TECHNOLOGICAL AND TECHNICAL TESTING GROUND OF THE OIL AND GAS INDUSTRY IN THE RUSSIAN FAR EAST"

Against the backdrop of strengthening sectoral sanctions and restrictions related to the Russian fuel and energy complex, in addition to the emerging strategic threat that hinders its long-term development, there is a need for import substitution of equipment in the fuel and energy complex and the transition of oil and gas companies to technological independence [13, 32]. At the same time, the implementation of a diversification turn, which activates the development of oil and gas fields in the eastern part of Russia, including the Russian Far East [13], generates a request from oil and gas projects for modern domestic technologies and equipment. For example, the Chayandinskoye oil and gas condensate field is a project where the widest range of technologies are implemented [33].

Considering such a request, as well as taking into account the other five strategic priorities developed and presented above, involving the implementation of large-scale projects with non-standard and advanced solutions, there is a need and a strategic opportunity to form a technological and technical testing ground for the gas industry in the Far Eastern Federal District.

The main goal of the strategic priority is the formation of an oil and gas scientific, technical, and innovative cluster that can act as a long-term technological and technical testing ground that provides both the internal needs of the industry and the possibility of exporting technologies and equipment.

As a competitive advantage, not only the presence and active participation in developing the industry of leading oil and gas companies in the Far Eastern Federal District is noted, but also their accumulated experience in cooperation and joint solutions with other leading companies (JSC "Atomenergomash," "HMS Group," "Severgroup," "Tyazhmash," "Rosatom," "Roskosmos," "Rostec," "Almaz-Antey Corporation," etc.) for the most important scientific and technological tasks [13]. Particular importance in the implementation of the strategic priority should be given to international cooperation.

Implementing this strategic priority will lead to the achievement of the most important societal effect associated with the development of human potential in the Far Eastern Federal District [34], which, first of all, is associated with the formation of an oil and gas scientific, technical, and innovation cluster, which includes the building of an effective scientific and educational system that contributes to the formation of the knowledge economy [35], and implies the organization of a system to train professional personnel.

From the point of view of budgetary (state) efficiency, the most important effect is to ensure strategic security in the field of oil and gas equipment, technologies, and software by leveling import dependence. The oil and gas scientific, technical, and innovation cluster in the Russian Far East will ensure the generation of innovative technological and technical developments, and their distribution and implementation will lead to a multiplied stimulation of the region's economic growth. The functioning of the technological and technical testing ground in the Far Eastern Federal District will strengthen interregional and international cooperation in the field of technological and technical development. The emerging technological and technical testing ground will act as an effective platform for the interaction of participants at different levels (state, regional, industrial, corporate, and international) to solve common scientific and technological problems in the oil and gas-related industries. Building an effective scientific and educational system on the basis of this test site, including a system for training professional personnel, will act as a point of attraction for young scientists and professional personnel, primarily Russian ones, to the Russian Far East, leveling the negative consequences of the "brain drain" and outflow of personnel.

Of the commercial effects, it is important to note the growth of investment attractiveness associated with the growth of innovative activity in the subjects of the Far Eastern Federal District, as well as the functioning of the oil and gas scientific, technical, and innovation cluster, which contributes to the development of highly qualified professional personnel in the oil and gas industry.

KEYWORDS

- **Asia-Pacific region**
- **gasification**
- **Russian Far East gas industry strategy**
- **strategic priority**
- **strategy mission concept**
- **strategy vision concept**
- **technical testing**

REFERENCES

1. Sasaev, (2021). Strategic diagnostics at the Russian Far East gas industry. *Russian Journal of Industrial Economics*, *14*(4), 355–368. https://doi.org/10.17073/2072-1633-2021-4-355-368 (In Russ.).
2. Ibid.
3. Filimonova, I. V., et al., (2019). Modern conditions and prospects for the development of gas resources in East Russia. *Mineral Recourses of Russia. Economics and Management*, *6*, 38–44.
4. Fadeev, A., Ilyinsky, A., & Ilyin, I., (2020). *The Development of the Sea of Okhotsk Shelf: Experience in Offshore Projects Development in Difficult Climatic Conditions Using the Example of PJSC Gazprom Neft* (Vol. T 539, No. 1, pp. C. 012168). IOP Publishing.
5. Sasaev, *Strategic Diagnostics at the Russian Far East Gas Industry.*
6. Marichev, S. G., (2021). Market attractiveness of oil and gas companies as a factor affecting the socio-economic development in regions of their business operations. *Economic Analysis: Theory and Practice*, *20*(1508), 124–141.
7. Sasaev, N. I., (2021). Strategizing of the Russian Far East gas industry: Systematization of main interests. *Strategizing: Theory and Practice, 1*(2), 242–251.
8. Sasaev, N. I., (2019). *Theoretical Foundations and Methodology of the Russian Gas Industry Development Strategy.* NWIM RANEPA.
9. Machakhova, A. K., (2015). Gas industry is a key driver of socio-economic development in the Republic of Sakha (Yakutia) (Russia, Yakutsk). *Problems of Modern Economics, 2*(54), 257–258.
10. Vladimir, L. K., & Vyacheslav, A. F., (2021). *The Fundamentals of Russia's Environmental Development Strategy*. Moscow University Press.
11. Sasaev, N. I., (2022). Sectoral strategy financing: strategic principles and efficiency. *The Economic Revival of Russia, 4*(70),77–87.
12. Sasaev, N. I., (2022). Strategic opportunities of the Russian Far East gas industry development: gasification, gas processing, and gas-chemistry. *Strategizing: Theory and Practice*, *2*(1), 106–118.
13. Sasaev, N. I., (2022). Strategic analysis of trends in the development of the Russian Far East gas industry. *Economic Analysis: Theory and Practice*, *21*(3), 416–441.
14. Sasaev, N. I., (2022). Network gas export is a strategic priority of the gas industry of the Russian Far East. *Russian Journal of Industrial Economics*, *15*(1), 17–25.
15. *The Fourteenth Five-Year Plan for the National Economic and Social Development of the People's Republic of China and the Outline of the Long-term Goals for 2035*, (2021). Gov.cn. http://www.gov.cn/xinwen/2021–03/13/content_5592681.htm (accessed on 3 January 2023).
16. *India's Greenhouse Gas Policy Is Driven by the Paris Agreement*, (2021). NG.ru. https://www.ng.ru/energy/2021-09-13/15_8250_india.html (accessed on 18 January 2024).
17. Ibid.
18. Makarova, Y. V., (2018). Global gas market development: The role of LNG. *Intellect. Innovation. Investments, 3*, 31–36.

19. *Shell LNG Outlook 2021*. Shell. https://www.shell.com/energy-and-innovation/natural-gas/liquefied-natural-gas-lng/lng-outlook-2021.html#iframe=L3dlYmFwcHMvTE5HX091dGxvb2svMjAyMS8 (accessed on 3 January 2023).
20. *High LNG Prices Put Spotlight on India's Exposure to Global Gas Market Volatility*, (2021). S&P Global. https://www.spglobal.com/platts/en/market-insights/latest-news/lng/101521-high-lng-prices-put-spotlight-on-indias-exposure-to-global-gas-market-volatility (accessed on 3 January 2023).
21. *NOVATEK Has Patented Its Own Natural Gas Liquefaction Technology Arctic Cascade*. Novatek. https://www.novatek.ru/ru/press/releases/index.php?id_4=2302 (accessed on 3 January 2023).
22. Naumov, Yu. A., (2020). On the features of air pollution in the Russian Far East. *Ojkumena. Regional Researches, 1*, 41–52.
23. *How the Russian Energy Balance Works*, (2021). RG.ru. https://rg.ru/2021/03/28/kak-ustroen-rossijskij-energeticheskij-balans.html (accessed on 3 January 2023).
24. The government approved a long-term program for the development of LNG production. Government.ru. http://government.ru/news/41790 (accessed on 3 January 2023).
25. Skaridov, A., (2021). "Green shipping" and the problem of sustainable use of maritime transport. *International Law and International Organizations, 1*, 31–45.
26. Almost 9.5 thousand tons of liquefied natural gas were produced at Gazprom Transgaz Yekaterinburg in 2021. Interfax Russia. https://www.interfax-russia.ru/ural/pressrel/v-2021-godu-v-gazprom-transgaz-ekaterinburg-proizvedeno-pochti-9-5-tysyach-tonn-szhizhennogo-prirodnogo-gaza (accessed on 18 January 2024).
27. Demina, O. V., & Dzhurka, N. G., (2020). Assessing the economic consequences of reducing emissions in the power supply system of the region: The experience of the Far East. *Regionalistics*, *7*(2), 5–23.
28. Belinskiy, A. V., (2018). Influence of the gas supply and the gas infrastructure development on the economic growth of regions of the Russian Federation (econometric approach). *GAS Industry of Russia, S2*(770).
29. Vyatkin, Yu. L., Lishchiner, I. I., Sinitsyn, S. A., & Kuzmin, A. M., (2020). *Prospective Directions of Chemical Processing of Hydrocarbon Raw Materials* (Vol. 4, No. 100, pp. 114–118). Neftegaz.ru.
30. The State of Gas Chemistry: The Energy Crisis Is Not a Hindrance—There Will Be Problems, But Not for Everyone, (2021). OilCapital.ru. https://oilcapital.ru/news/2021-10-15/sostoyanie-gazohimii-energokrizis-ne-pomeha-problemy-budut-no-ne-u-vseh-1043132 (accessed on 18 January 2024).
31. Ibid.
32. Fadeev, A. M., (2022). Energy projects in the Arctic: Strategic priorities of technological independence. *Strategizing: Theory and Practice, 2*(1), 88–105.
33. Davydov, A. V., et al., (2017). Chayandinskoye field is the project of new technologies implementation in East Siberia. *Perm Journal of Petroleum and Mining Engineering, 16*(2), 113–128.
34. Novikova, I. V., (2020). *The Russian Far East: Strategic Development of the Workforce*. Apple Academic Press.
35. Makarov, V. L., (2004). Knowledge economy: Lessons for Russia. *Russia and the Contemporary World, 1*(42), 5–24.

Conclusion

In non-stationary economic conditions, it becomes strategically important to search for and justify potential drivers for a breakthrough in the socio-economic development of the Far Eastern Federal District—one of the most promising Russian macro-regions.

The results of a comprehensive strategic analysis reveal that the Russian Far East gas industry can act as a potential driver, on which the entire spectrum of interests is concentrated through its development and functioning, and which has a number of large-scale strategic opportunities. Based on this, this monograph forms the Russian Far East gas industry strategy (mission and vision), revealing the resource and technological potential of the region.

The author presents in detail six concepts of the FEFD gas industry's main strategic priorities, the synchronous and complete implementation of which will lead to developing the gas industry as one of the drivers of the FEFD's socio-economic development in the long term, providing a whole spectrum of interests (national, public, regional, industrial, corporate, and international), and generating a wide range of public and economic multiplicative effects.

Strategizing the Russian Gas Industry: The Far Eastern Vector. Nikita I. Sasaev (Ed)

Index

F

H

I

M

N

O

T

U

For Product Safety Concerns and Information please contact our
EU representative GPSR@taylorandfrancis.com Taylor & Francis
Verlag GmbH, Kaufingerstraße 24, 80331 München, Germany